AS I SAID

Lev Loseff
AS I SAID
КАК Я СКАЗАЛ

☙

Translated by
G. S. Smith

Introduced by
Barry P. Scherr

2012

Published by Arc Publications,
Nanholme Mill, Shaw Wood Road
Todmorden OL14 6DA, UK
www.arcpublications.co.uk

Original poems copyright © Estate of Lev Loseff 2012
Translation copyright © G. S. Smith 2012
Introduction copyright © Barry P. Scherr 2012
Copyright in the present edition © Arc Publications, 2012

Design by Tony Ward
Printed in Great Britain by the
MPG Books Group, Bodmin & King's Lynn

978 1904614 83 8 (pbk)
978 1906570 11 8 (hbk)

ACKNOWLEDGEMENTS
Earlier versions of some of these translations were published in *The Dark Horse*, *The Oxford Magazine*, *Poetry Review*, and *The Times Literary Supplement*

Cover painting by Marcus Ward

This book is in copyright. Subject to statutory exception and to provision of relevant collective licensing agreements, no reproduction of any part of this book may take place without the written permission of Arc Publications

**Arc Publications: 'Visible Poets' series
Editor: Jean Boase-Beier**

CONTENTS

Series Editor's Note / 9
Translator's Preface / 10
Introduction / 16

24 / В клинике • At the Clinic / 25

Говорящий попугай / The Talking Parrot

26 / Квартира • The Flat / 27
26 / Экскурсия • An Excursion / 27
28 / Казань, июль 1957 • Kazan, July 1957 / 29
30 / Школа № 1 • School No. 1 / 31
30 / Козлищ как не • Who Says Sheep Are
приравняешь к овцам? Different From Goats? / 31
32 / Иосиф в 1965 году • Joseph in 1965 / 33
34 / Депрессия-Россия • Russian Depression / 35
36 / В пустом зале • In the Empty Room / 37

Как я сказал / As I Said

38 / Замывание крови.... • The Blood Washed Off.... / 39
38 / Новоселье • The New Abode / 39
42 / Опять нелетная погода • Grounded Again / 43
42 / Памяти полярника • In Memory of a Polar
Explorer / 43
44 / Прозрачный дом • The See-through House / 45
44 / В похоронном дому... • The Funeral Parlour's Abuzz... / 45
46 / С.Д. • S. D. / 47
48 / Из Бунина • Out of Bunin / 49
48 / Отрывок • Fragment / 49
50 / Пирс испарился • The Pier that Disappeared / 51
52 / Под старость... • As You Get On... / 53
54 / Город живет... • This City's Alive... / 55
54 / Сейчас • Right Now / 55

Sisyphus Redux

58 / Июнь 1972 года • June 1972 / 59
60 / Почерк Достоевского • Dostoevsky's Handwriting / 61

60 / Реформатор • The Reformer / 61
62 / Стоп-кадр • Freeze-frame / 63

Послесловие / Afterword

66 / Послесловие • Afterword / 67
80 / Памяти Михаила Красильникова • In Memory of Mikhail Krasilnikov / 81
82 / «Я и старая дама» • Me and the Old Lady / 83
84 / Сердцебиение • Heartbeat / 85

Новые сведения о Карле и Кларе / New Information concerning Carl and Clara

86 / Нет • Not / 87
86 / Без названия • Untitled / 87
88 / Ветхая осень • Old Testament Autumn / 89
88 / В альбом О. • For O's Scrapbook / 89
90 / Забытые деревни • Forgotten Villages / 91
92 / Джентрификация • Gentrification / 93
94 / Парижская нота • The Parisian Note / 95
96 / Подражание • Imitation / 97
96 / С грехом пополам • There but for… / 97

Тайный советник / Privy Councillor

102 / Апрель 1950 • April 1950 / 103
102 / Туалет • Toilette / 103
104 / В гроссбух • Ledger Entry / 105
106 / Декабрьские дикие сны • December Dreams Come in a Crazy Rush / 107
108 / Разбужен неожиданной тишиной • Awakened by an Unexpected Silence / 109

Чудесный десант / The Miraculous Raid

110 / Местоимения • Pronouns / 111
112 / Трамвай • The Tram / 113
114 / Живу в Америке от скуки • I'm Living in the States From Boredom / 115

116 / Тем и прекрасны • The splendid thing about
        эти сны   these dreams / 117
118 / Земную жизнь пройдя • Having traversed half my
        до середины   three score and ten / 119
122 / Сонет • Sonnet / 123
124 / Продленный день... • The Extended Day... / 125
138 / Нелетная погода • Grounded / 139
142 / Последний романс • The Last Romance / 143
144 / Он говорил: ‹А это • 'And this one here is basil',
        базилик›   he declared / 145

Author's & Translator's Notes / 146

Biographical Notes / 153

SERIES EDITOR'S NOTE

The 'Visible Poets' series was established in 2000, and set out to challenge the view that translated poetry could or should be read without regard to the process of translation it had undergone. Since then, things have moved on. Today there is more translated poetry available and more debate on its nature, its status, and its relation to its original. We know that translated poetry is neither English poetry that has mysteriously arisen from a hidden foreign source, nor is it foreign poetry that has silently rewritten itself in English. We are more aware that translation lies at the heart of all our cultural exchange; without it, we must remain artistically and intellectually insular.

One of the aims of the series was, and still is, to enrich our poetry with the very best work that has appeared elsewhere in the world. And the poetry-reading public is now more aware than it was at the start of this century that translation cannot simply be done by anyone with two languages. The translation of poetry is a creative act, and translated poetry stands or falls on the strength of the poet-translator's art. For this reason 'Visible Poets' publishes only the work of the best translators, and gives each of them space, in a Preface, to talk about the trials and pleasures of their work.

From the start, 'Visible Poets' books have been bilingual. Many readers will not speak the languages of the original poetry but they, too, are invited to compare the look and shape of the English poems with the originals. Those who can are encouraged to read both. Translation and original are presented side-by-side because translations do not displace the originals; they shed new light on them and are in turn themselves illuminated by the presence of their source poems. By drawing the readers' attention to the act of translation itself, it is the aim of these books to make the work of both the original poets and their translators more visible.

Jean Boase-Beier

TRANSLATOR'S PREFACE

The translations in this book are authorised, which needs some explanation. The most familiar use of the word occurs, of course, in connection with the King James Bible, and is intended as a minatory indication of doctrinal correctness: the authorities are stating that this is *the* translation, and the faithful must spurn all others. It goes without saying that I intend nothing of this sort; in fact, I hope that among other things the appearance of these versions of Lev Loseff's poetry will encourage other translators to tackle it. What I wish to convey is the main fact about these translations that for me makes them different from any other verse texts I have undertaken: they were developed in consultation with the author and were granted his approval.

In the present state of copyright law as I understand it, one may not simply go ahead and publish translations of the work of a living author without that author's permission, and in this sense all legal translations are authorised. Concerning the translations in this book I am speaking about something more than this kind of permission. Most living authors or their agents, I would guess, grateful for the attention and the possible proceeds, freely grant permission for translation and do not vet the results; apart from anything else, they probably lack the linguistic competence to make a well-founded judgement. In this respect Loseff was different, in fact perhaps in a class of his own. Of all the literary Russians I have encountered in over forty years of professional activity in the field, he had the most profound and subtle knowledge of English, and so his comments carried weight.

I say this in full awareness – an unavoidable and even forbidding awareness – of the poet who not so long ago radically changed the situation with regard to the translation of Russian poetry into English. Joseph Brodsky happened to be one of Loseff's closest friends, and Loseff wrote both a biography of him and extensive annotations for the most authoritative Russian edition of his poetry. In these writings, he on the whole avoided analysing the linguistic aspect of the work Brodsky wrote in English, translated and original, for the good reason that his priorities lay elsewhere – in the centrally important questions of the life and primary writings of his subject. The work of what is by now a substantial number of scholars has shown, though, that Brodsky wished increasingly to control the translation of his work into English. The translated texts of his poems begin by being attributed unambiguously to someone else, then comes a period when they are attributed to Brodsky jointly with a collaborator, and eventually we find what some people have called auto-translations, with Brodsky credited as both author and translator. I am inclined to think that these latter texts belong to a specific genre that merits analysis separately from translations made by more familiar methods; whatever be the case, they are 'authorised' in a much stricter sense than the way I wish to imply with regard to my version of Loseff.

Brodsky used to insist that his Russian poetry be translated into an English that reflects the verse form of the original. I say this as the grateful one-time recipient of his permission to break this rule. When I put together my bilingual anthology *Contemporary Russian Poetry* in the late 1980s, the model I had in mind was Dimitri Obolensky's *Penguin Book of Russian Verse* (1962), the book from which I and my generation of Russianists gained our basic knowledge of the subject. My anthology was eventually published in 1993, and gratefully dedicated to Obolensky. The prose translations in that Penguin reader, appended at the bottom of the page according to the standard format for the series in which it appeared, were apart from anything else a treasure trove for Anglophone students of Russian. I wanted to pursue the same pedagogical objective in my anthology, though I preferred *en-face* translations that mirrored the line divisions of the original. I asked Brodsky for permission to print this kind of translation of the ten poems of his I had chosen, arguing that the anthology would simply be invalid without his presence, but also that a deviation from the standard format would seriously damage the integrity of the book; and he gave permission for my versions without challenging my selection or demanding to vet the results.

My first substantial batch of translations of Lev Loseff's

poetry was made for this same anthology. In a survey article of 1987 that outlined the situation in Russian poetry my anthology later tried to represent, I published a couple of metrical translations of poems by him, and the following year I published an article entirely devoted to his work. I then set about the translations for my anthology, consulting the author as I went. I still have the earliest drafts I sent Loseff, returned with extensive but crisp annotations in his precise handwriting. Not for nothing was he at one time a professional editor, on the Leningrad journal *Kostër (The Campfire),* and later at Ardis publishers, where he edited two of Brodsky's major collections. I realised then that not only did he possess an extraordinarily nuanced comprehension of my sometimes excessively colloquial English English, but also was capable of explicating his own work to an extent I had not encountered before among Russian poets. Even more, he was willing to do so, and to an outsider to boot, without retreating into obscurantism or protestations of professional tradecraft. I was not surprised by this capacity; it went hand in hand with the exceptionally high intellectual level of Loseff's poetry and also his self-deprecating attitudes. One respect in which Loseff repeatedly drew a line and preferred not to explicate, though, was in the matter of annotation. At my request, he provided the notes appended to the English texts below, but he was unwilling to have some cryptic references explained, for example certain initials, preferring not to make the text so specific, and more generally not to spoonfeed the reader; and I have perforce respected his preferences.

One very important respect in which the present text is not authorised in the familiar sense concerns the choice of texts for translation. This choice has been entirely mine, and not surprisingly I have gone for those poems that seemed to me to work well in English. Lev Loseff did not offer very many comments on my choices, and several years ago he declined my invitation to draw up a list of what would seem to him essential if the selection were to be representative according to his own view of his work. I became convinced after many vain attempts that a substantial proportion of what he wrote defies adequate translation, or at least defies my capacity for it. Even though I believe that in principle everything and anything can be translated if the right method can be found, I challenge anyone to English those supremely witty poems by Loseff where Russian wordplay is both the principal device and the subject matter, functioning as both form and content. Just one such is 'Son o iunosti' ('Dreaming about my Youth') from the collection *Posleslovie* (*Afterword*, 1998), where Loseff makes hilarious and simultaneously poignant common nouns out of the names of his youthful pals. Faced with lacunae such as this, all I can do is offer an impression of how much is here and how much has been omitted: I would guess that in all, this book offers versions of about a quarter of the total original œuvre. The reverse chronological order by published collection adopted in this book, though, unlike the selection of poems, reflects the author's strongly declared preference, which I never felt entitled to question.

One of the poems I chose for my 1993 anthology was Loseff's characteristically wry account of his experience as a professional editor in Russia. My painful awareness of the elegance and packed economy that was lost from his metrical Russian in my prose version was the most powerful stimulus for my attempts to make translations in verse. Elegance is one thing, economy another; or perhaps not, when translation is the subject. In speaking about these qualities, though, the spectre arises of the most unavoidable and intractable problem faced by translators of Russian poetry: formal equivalence, and the entailed pressure to add to or subtract from the original. Even highly sophisticated Russians in my experience tend to believe that broadly speaking, Western poetry, and poetry in English in particular, has abandoned strict form, whereas their own has remained true to it and is better off as a result. In my opinion this belief both seriously underestimates the persistence and perceived validity of strict form in English, and equally seriously misunderstands the dynamic nature of the Russian treatment of it. To refer to Russian metrical practice as 'traditional' (or even worse, 'conservative' or 'classical') is woefully misleading. For Russian poets writing in the early twenty-first century it is in no sense odd or archaic to believe, for example, that iambic and trochaic metres are palpably different in their semantic and stylistic associations, and so on across the entire repertoire of metrical resources, including rhyme. And so the translator constantly needs to weigh how best to proceed in representing this repertoire, one that has indeed been largely eroded in front-line poetry in English over the last hundred years. This problem is particularly important for the translator of Loseff, who has a virtuoso command of the entire spectrum of received metrical forms (and has added a few of his own) in addition to an extraordinarily acute understanding of their historical resonances.

However the translator proceeds, the fact remains that apart from the broad distinction between strict and free form, particular verse forms have different, historically conditioned, associations in different national traditions. And so if I grasp at what seems like a particularly helpful straw and gratefully slip into English iambic pentameter when Loseff uses this line in his Russian, I must do so in the awareness that what for once seems like one-to-one equivalence is in fact misleading. To summarize: English iambic pentameter goes back to the Middle Ages and includes Shakespeare's blank verse, while Russian iambic pentameter goes back no further than the first decade of the nineteenth century, is almost always rhymed, and is neither Pushkin's principal metre nor closely associated with dramatic verse; and this is to say nothing of the differences between the rhythmical variations that occur when the two languages are made to fit into this formal matrix. Some knowing translators of Russian poetry into English have concluded that in this situation they should abandon the original and perhaps even go for free form, but that is not my choice. For one thing, one had better be a serious original poet in English to act in this way with any authority, and I am not one. The most I can do is to try and capture as much as I can of what the original actually says, while also conveying some idea of how it is made; the strangeness that sometimes results is to me a benefit, something that accords with the subject matter.

I have no quarrel with the English poets who have enriched our understanding of foreign poetry by substituting their own versification for that of the original; their versions have their own value. I also admire another instructive exploration of this problem, this time by a scholar: M. L. Gasparov once re-translated into free verse some of the metrical translations of various foreign classics made over the years by Russian poets working from prose cribs, demonstratively stripping them of the padding and syntactic distortion that Russian strict-form practice had introduced. Perhaps I should simply say that the distinction between verse and poetry is drawn in a different way in Russian than it is in English. I have written a good deal about this bundle of issues elsewhere, though, and would prefer to say no more about it here, instead leaving the reader to form an independent judgement about my method and its results.

Finally, I would like to pay tribute to Lev Loseff especially for his patience and forbearance during the many years I consulted with him, and to say that I hope he felt at least some of the gratification I experienced in working towards a result that I am proud to call 'authorised' in the sense I outlined above.

G. S. Smith

INTRODUCTION

Lev Loseff is a poet's poet – or at least a lover of poetry's poet. While some of his poems exhibit a playful quality, with their punning and humorous observations, his writing tends on the whole to be complex in its imagery, rich in literary allusion, and abundant in formal experiment. A highly intellectual poetry, it reflects his immersion in Russian culture as a young man growing up in Soviet Russia, but also the distance and range of experience provided by emigration: having turned to poetry in 1974, he left for the United States two years later. Thus the vast majority of his work was written abroad as he contemplated his native land from both a literal and a figurative distance, while at the same time casting a sometimes jaundiced eye on the alien culture in which he spent the final thirty-three years of his life.

Virtually every biographical note on Lev Loseff begins by pointing out that he began to write serious poetry only at age 37, both a very late age for any poet to start and also the age at which Pushkin, Russia's greatest poet, died following a duel. Since he was born in the fateful year 1937, when Stalin's purges were to attain their full intensity, that means he began to write when he had attained the age of his birth year in the century. Possibly, then, the very symbolism of "37" was as important a factor in his deciding to write poetry as others that he cited – recovery from an illness that had caused him to reflect on life, the departure of his close friend Joseph Brodsky to the West in 1972, and a sense that the acquaintances of his younger years were growing more distant.

Be that as it may, there was much in his surroundings to draw him to literature. He not only had a well-known poet for a father, but his circle of close friends when he attended Leningrad University included Mikhail Yeremin, Sergei Kulle, Vladimir Ufliand, and Leonid Vinogradov, all of whom were to become writers. They, along with Aleksandr Kondratov (who was not at the university), and the slightly older Mikhail Krasilnikov and Yuri Mikhailov, comprised what eventually became known as the "philological school" of Russian poets. The name seems to derive from Leningrad University's Philology Faculty, where the majority of them studied. However, other than their mutual friendship and a penchant for experimentation in their verse, little suggests that they ever formed a unified group. As it turns out, Kulle's free verse, Vinogradov's brief aphoristic poems and Kondratov's conceptual poetry all are further from the mainstream literary traditions than is Loseff, who has also referred to Gleb Gorbovskii, Yevgeny Rein and, of course, Joseph Brodsky as poets whom he knew well in his younger years. However accurate the name or even the notion that the eight writers comprised a school, the term "philological poet" seems appropriate for Lev Loseff. He achieved an intimate familiarity with the whole of the Russian poetic tradition to which he refers regularly in his verse. If he feels any "anxiety of influence," he does not show it, except perhaps in relation to Brodsky. As he notes in his introduction to the collection *Afterword*, which appears in this volume (see 'Notes', p. 147), for many years he consciously avoided allowing any Brodskian elements into his own writing. Then the floodgates opened after Brodsky's death in 1996, when he wrote an entire cycle of poems linked to the memory of his close friend. Ten of the sixteen works in that cycle are included here. Other acquaintances from his youth turn up in his poetry as well: the poem 'In Memory of Mikhail Krasilnikov' (p. 81) recalls the figure whom Loseff and his friends regarded as their inspiration, while many of his poet friends are referred to in dedications or make cameo appearances within the bodies of poems. But he hardly limits himself to authors from that narrow circle. Within the generous sampling of his verse included in this volume, Loseff mentions other poets of his day – Yevtushenko, Glazkov, Okudzhava – and refers to several from earlier in the twentieth century: Blok, Gumilev, Pasternak. Among nineteenth-century poets, Pushkin, Zhukovsky, Lermontov, Fedor Glinka and Polonsky (in the epigraph to 'Heartbeat', p. 85) are all cited. And his range of interests extends beyond Russia: Marianne Moore appears in 'Right Now' (p. 55) while 'The Parisian Note' (p. 95) quotes Verlaine. And, not limiting himself to poetry, Loseff has a poem ('Out of Bunin', p. 49) inspired by Bunin's powerful story 'Light Breathing' and another lyric on Dostoevsky. Nor do these names exhaust the list of those who were important to him. When Brodsky first read Loseff's verse he was most of all reminded of the early nineteenth-century poet Konstantin Batiushkov, while others have noted similarities between his work and that of an earlier émigré writer, Vladislav Khodasevich. The early poem 'Lefloseff' refers to several figures he admired, including Tsvetaeva, Mandelshtam, and Khlebnikov. (This is one of the works that G. S. Smith has in mind in his introduction when he speaks of poems defying translation; Loseff refers to each of the three poets by words derived from their first names, for instance calling himself a "marinist," which in Russian literally means a painter of seascapes, but in this instance refers to a person who studies Marina [Tsvetaeva]).

In short, Lev Loseff was profoundly absorbed in the world of literature, but at the same time the inspiration for individual works arose from real-life experiences. He was, first of all, a poet of Leningrad, and referred to himself as a native of that city, not of the St. Petersburg that came before and after his time there. Indeed, the longer he lived in the United States, for all his attachment to Russian culture, he saw New England as his home and, even when it became politically possible, never returned to his birth city, which for him no longer existed outside his mind's eye. Thus in many of his poems he evokes the Soviet era, most often recalling the Leningrad of his youth as in his early 'The Tram' (p. 113), where that fateful conjunction of 3 and 7 appears once again, or in the more recent and if anything even darker 'An Excursion' (p. 27) which revisits the district in which he grew up.

Much of his most compelling poetry coalesces from the detritus of memory, which he scrutinizes and prods with all the determination of an archaeologist exploring the remnants of a dead civilization. 'Kazan, July 1957' (p. 29), another of his newer poems, is typical in this regard: the recollection of a crippled soldier, begging for bread, emerges from something "yellowy-violet," at first indeterminate, perhaps a flower, but later, after the unseeing left eye comes to mind, transformed into the yellowy-violet left cheek of the invalid's face. There is something unflinching and merciless in the way that Loseff displays that which most would prefer to keep forgotten or hidden away. Brodsky, in saying that Loseff's poetry reminded him of Batiushkov's, said that it did so because both were poets of restraint. No doubt Brodsky had in mind the relatively emotionless effect of the lyric narrator and the classical forms to which Loseff adhered in most of his poetry. However, the seemingly quiet manner only served to mask the ultimate power of his verse. Whether resurrecting his own past, casting a cold eye on the present or musing on more abstract topics, Loseff would conjure up a restless and frequently disturbing universe.

He was, ultimately, a poet of observation. His verse conveys emotion – fear, a sense of loss, bemusement – but it is emotion that arises from contemplating the world outside the poet, rather than the writer's most intimate thoughts. Even when Loseff appears within his own works, he does so as an observer or as the observed, often with an ironic detachment on the part of the narrator. Nowhere is this clearer than in 'At the Clinic' (p. 25), one of his last poems, describing the moment when he receives the fatal prognosis from his doctor. It is almost as though the poet is standing outside himself, looking at and feeling sorry for the physician at the same time as scrutinizing his own surprisingly calm reaction. Given his penchant for looking at his subjects from without, he not surprisingly avoided writing directly about love or about his inner desires: perhaps this too is one of the qualities that caused Brodsky to emphasize his restraint.

This very quality leads to some of the difficulty in fully grasping his poetry. Emotions tend toward the universal; observation toward the specific and the exceptional. To follow his eye's path and the reasoning to which his gaze gives rise requires an understanding of the context and the object. While his poems contain many minor biographical details, what is of far greater importance is the awareness of the Soviet society in which he grew up, of the history that turned St. Petersburg into Leningrad and back into St. Petersburg, and of the literary tradition that he knew intimately and that informed much of his work.

Striving to understand the meaning of his poems should not cause readers to neglect his technical virtuosity. He was a master of verse form, who managed to innovate even while displaying many of the classical features found in earlier Russian poetry. While some of his artistry comes through only in the Russian, the translations in this volume manage to convey much of the structural richness and variety. Take 'Freeze-frame' (p. 63), a poem from the collection *Sisyphus Redux*. Each group of three lines is connected by rhyme, creating an unusual stanza, rhyming a a a. But the stanza form is maintained only for the first two stanzas, and then is re-established for the final three lines of this fifteen-line poem. Lines 7-12 are divided into units of two, two-and-a-half, and one-and-a-half lines, so that there is a disjunction between the semantic structure of the poem and the units created by the rhyme. This lack of symmetry helps single out the passage describing the world that appears after the narrator's Faustian encounter. The feeling of imbalance and asymmetry receives emphasis from the use of enjambement, particularly between lines 6 and 7, where the syntax leaps across the boundary between stanzas. Rich sound play occurs throughout the poem, with the English "hiss", "hot" and "horrendous" in the sixth line offering a reflection of what takes place in the original. The Russian text turns out to be still more complex. The very long lines are composed in dactylic heptameter, with the fourth foot consistently "missing" a syllable at the point of the caesura. What is more, the last words in the fourth feet form triple "internal" rhymes themselves, though in this case the rhymes are feminine, with the rhyme vowel in the penultimate syllable. So it could be said that each seven-foot line consists of a dactylic tetrameter, with one syllable truncated, followed by a dactylic trimeter. In short, the poem is written in a highly complex and possibly unique metrical form, only a hint of which can be conveyed in English.

Of course, not all the poems attain this level of complexity, but time and again formal features will turn out to be notable, sometimes for their sheer inventiveness, but often as well for the way in which they help structure the work and help emphasize key images or ideas. Take 'An Excursion' (p. 27), one of Loseff's late poems, written in the familiar iambic pentameter, but in a seven-line stanza (less common in Russian than in English, where Chaucer and Byron both used it). The rhyme scheme is a a B c c a B, where the capital letters indicate feminine rhymes. The metre and the stanza form are conveyed precisely in the English, as is the play with non-Russian words in the first line of the last stanza. Some of the sound quality comes across as well: "Sodom" in line 1, followed by "So down" in line 2 imitates almost exactly what takes place in the Russian. Other effects are harder to get across. Line 2 in the second stanza consists entirely of very "Soviet" abbreviations (for example, *narsud* for *narodnyyi sud* or people's court), which reflect a linguistic trait of the era in which this poem is set. A special effect marks the last line in each stanza: an extra foot, a highly symmetrical syntactical structure, and a near-rhyme of the two main nouns in line 7; extraordinary sound play in line 14 (with a stressed "u" in four consecutive words; "tr" beginning three words and "dr" two others); and in line 21 the Russian word for Hell appearing on a syllable that would normally be left unstressed, so that the occurrence of two consecutive stressed syllables (followed by an unstressed syllable where stress would be expected) leads to a disjointed rhythm and emphasizes "Hell" all the more strongly.

And sometimes it is simply worth noting one or two less elaborate features, such as in the much earlier 'Ledger Entry' (p. 105), where the last line is in trimeter, providing an effective closure to this iambic tetrameter poem, while the couplets in masculine rhyme throughout the work create a kind of lilting effect, which is in keeping with the work's relatively light mood.

Perhaps the semantic and the formal intricacy of Lev Loseff's verse explains why until now only a few poems have been published in English, and most of those by the same G. S. Smith who is responsible for this volume. Loseff was a challenging poet, not only for the would-be translator, but also for the reader in any language. Highly original in their structure as well as their content, the poems repay a careful study that brings to the surface the hidden meanings and effects. Over the years Lev Loseff gradually became recognized among Russians as one of the leading poets of his era; now, with the generous selection of his verse provided in *As I Said*, Anglophone readers will have the opportunity to discover for themselves his distinctive and ever inventive voice.

Barry P. Scherr

AS I SAID
КАК Я СКАЗАЛ

В КЛИНИКЕ

Мне доктор что-то бормотал про почку
и прятал взгляд. Мне было жаль врача.
Я думал: жизнь прорвала оболочку
и потекла, легка и горяча.

Диплом на стенке. Врач. Его неловкость.
Косой рецепт строчащая рука.
А я дивился: о, какая легкость,
как оказалась эта весть легка!

Где демоны, что век за мной гонялись?
Я новым, легким воздухом дышу.
Сейчас пойду, и кровь сдам на анализ,
и эти строчки кровью подпишу.

AT THE CLINIC

The doctor mumbled things about my kidneys,
and looked away. I pitied this MD.
For life to me had burst its inhibitions,
and now flowed heatedly and easily.

Diploma on the wall. MD. His awkward silence.
Hand scribbling out a slanting recipe.
While I'm astonished by this easy lightness –
so easy had the news turned out to be!

What happened to the demons that beset me?
I'm breathing easily, not like before.
I'll go and let them have some blood for testing,
and give a bit more blood to sign this poem.

I
Из книги
ГОВОРЯЩИЙ ПОПУГАЙ (2010)

КВАРТИРА

Мне приснилась квартира окном на дворец и Неву,
на иглу золотую, что присниться могла б наркоману.
Мне сначала приснилось: я в этой квартире живу.
Но потом мне приснилось, что мне это не по карману.

Мне приснилось (со злобой), что здесь будет жить
вор-чиновник, придворная челядь, бандитская нелюдь
иль попсовая тварь. Мне приснилось: пора уходить.
Но потом мне приснилось, что можно ведь сон переделать.

И тогда в этом сне я снова протопал к окну
и увидел внизу облака, купола золотые и шпили,
и тогда в этом сне мне приснилось, что здесь и усну,
потому что так высоко, а лифта еще не пустили.

ЭКСКУРСИЯ

Вот наш водитель объявил: «Содом».
Сойдем. Осмотримся. Зайдем
в кинотеатр. Милуются мужчины,
и пахнет семенем. И нет свободных мест.
А на экране свалка и инцест,
седалищем, влагалищем и ртом
тот ест собачину, та просит мертвечины.

I
from
THE TALKING PARROT (2010)

THE FLAT

I dreamed of a flat looking out on the palace, on the Neva,
on that golden needle a junkie might see in his dreams.
At first I dreamed I was living here, in this flat.
But then I dreamed that this place was beyond my means.

I dreamed (getting riled) that in this place there would live
thieving bureaucrats, lickspittle courtiers, criminal scum,
or pop-music trash. I dreamed it was time to leave.
But then I dreamed that a dream may well be redone.

And then in this dream I went to the window once more,
and beneath me saw clouds, and golden domes and spires,
and then in this dream I dreamed I would fall asleep here,
being so high up, with the lift still not authorised.

AN EXCURSION

'We're here! Welcome to Sodom,' calls our guide.
So down we get, look round; then we're inside
a cinema. Men pleasuring themselves,
the smell of semen. Not one seat is free.
Gangbang and incest up there on the screen,
per rectum and per vulvum; gaping wide,
he goes for dogmeat, she dead human flesh.

Вот едем дальше. Остановка «Ад».
Нарсуд. Военкомат. Химкомбинат.
Над дохлой речкой испускают трубы
смердящий сероводородом дым.
Здесь небо не бывает голубым.
Оранжев дым, закат коричневат.
В трамвае друг о дружку трутся трупы.

Voilà un garçon, ein Knabe, a boy.
Из школы с окровавленной губой,
без букваря, без ранца, без пенала,
без шапки, без надежды, без души.
Вот медленно плывут карандаши –
зеленый, желтый, красный, голубой –
водой Ад обводящего канала.

КАЗАНЬ, ИЮЛЬ 1957

Толстые мухи. Столовая.
«Выдача блюд до шести».
Мелкое, желто-лиловое
тщится на клумбе расти.

Парализованный, в кителе,
тычется в бок инвалид.
«Вытери»? – Нет, вроде, «выдели».
«Выдели хлеба», – велит.

Хлеб отдаю, недоеденный,
желтое пиво, азу.
Смотрит он белой отметиной
в левом незрячем глазу.

The next stop on our trip is known as Hell.
Courthouse, recruiting office, rancid smell –
hydrogen sulphide fumes, smokestacked away
from a chemical plant above a putrid stream.
This is a place where blue sky's never been.
Orange the fumes and dun the sunset pall.
Corpses riding a tram jostle and sway.

Voilà un garçon, Knabe, little lad.
On his way home from school, lip smudged with blood;
no vocab book, no pencil case, no satchel,
no cap, no hope, and no immortal soul.
His pencils float away, so very slow –
the green, the blue, the yellow, and the red –
on the waters of Hell's boundary canal.

KAZAN, JULY 1957

Public canteen. Bloated flies.
'After 6 pm no food served'.
Bushes, with something yellowy-violet
that isn't going to survive.

A palsied veteran, still in army gear,
pokes a finger in my ribs.
'Scare'? No, it could be 'spare'.
'Spare some bread', he raps.

I let this Deadeye have the bread
left over, and some yellow beer.
He watches with the white bead
he has for a left eye; it can't see.

Видимо, слабо кумекая,
тянется вилкой к борщу.
Вот уже чуть не полвека я
все за собою тащу

тусклую память, готовую
мне подставлять без конца
мертвую, желто-лиловую
левую щеку лица.

ШКОЛА № 1

Брюхатый поп широким махом
за труповозкою кадит.
Лепечет скрученный бандит:
«Я не стрелял, клянусь Аллахом».
Вливается в пробои свет,
задерживается на детях, женщинах,
их тряпках, их мозгах, кишечниках.
Он ищет Бога. Бога нет.

КОЗЛИЩ КАК НЕ ПРИРАВНЯЕШЬ К ОВЦАМ?

Козлищ как не приравняешь к овцам?
Что-то есть военное в церковном.
Ризы, пригвожденные к иконам,
отливают золотом погонным.

Словно в блиндаже фитиль огарка.
Меньше света от него, чем чада.

Not quite all there, apparently,
he reaches for his borshch using a fork.
It's nigh on half a century,
and to this day I still backpack

this memory that won't entirely fade;
it proffers endlessly inside my head
the left cheek of a face –
yellowy-violet, and dead.

SCHOOL NO. 1

A big-bellied priest censering bodily
behind the corpse carrier.
And a trussed-up ruffian babbling
'I didn't shoot, I swear by Allah'.
Light streams in through the breaches,
lingers on children, women, on
their rags, their entrails, their brains.
Looking for God. There is no God.

WHO SAYS SHEEP ARE DIFFERENT FROM GOATS?

Who says sheep are different from goats?
Church and Army have their communalities.
– Those vestments tacked to icons, their gold
glittering like epaulettes.

You could be in a dugout: candle stub
whose wick gives off more soot than light;

Роспись на стене дрожит, как карта,
где кольцо сжимают силы Ада.

Золотого купола редиска.
Звонницы издерганные нервы.
Пономарь с косичкой, как радистка.
«Первый! Шлите подкрепленье! Первый?»

Для чего еще духовным лицам
лбами прикасаться к половицам,
если им не чудится оттуда
приближенье рокота и гуда.

Подползают к храму иномарки,
неотвратные, как танки НАТО.

Бабки тушат пальцами огарки.

Кто их знает, может, так и надо?

ИОСИФ В 1965 ГОДУ

Вся эта сволочь с партактивами
цветок за цвет и за мерцание
звезду могла бы сжить со света.

Стихов «с гражданскими мотивами»
потребовали от поэта.

Но в результате замерзания
в его чернильнице чернил
стихов с гражданскими мотивами
поэт для них не сочинил.

frescoes shimmering like a campaign map,
the hosts of Hell closing in tight.

Golden cupola like a radio dish.
Jangled nerves from the bell tower.
Pigtailed sexton like a signals miss:
'Come in, HQ! Send backup! Over?'

Why should persons of the cloth
do that forehead-floorboard pose
unless they catch, rising from beneath,
the clang of caterpillars coming close?

Foreign limos creeping up to churches,
inexorable as the tanks of NATO.

Candle stubs an old hag finger-pinches.

Who knows, maybe that's the way to go.

JOSEPH IN 1965

Those Party activists were bloody-minded
enough to hound a flower for its fragrance
or a star for its twinkle.

From the poet they demanded
poems 'with civic resonance'.

But in that ultimate inkwell
it made the fluid freeze into black ice;
for them this poet refused to make
poems with civic resonance.

Он слушал сердца замирания,
следил за кряквами крикливыми
и крыши драные чинил.

Река плела свои извивы.
Шёл снег. Стояли холода.
И, как гражданские мотивы,
чего-то ныли провода.

ДЕПРЕССИЯ-РОССИЯ
Е. Р.

Вся Россия, от среднего пояса
с бездорожьем туды и сюды
и до Арктики, аж до полюса,
где подтаивать начали льды,

финский дождик, без устали сеющий,
жаркий луч на таврическом льве
уместились в седой и лысеющей
черноглазой твоей голове.

Эту хворь тебе наулюлюкали
Блок да Хлебников, с них и ответ.
В ней московский, с истерикой, с глюками,
в январе эйфорический бред

и унынье в июне, депрессия,
в стенку взгляд в петербургской норе,
и чудесный момент равновесия
на тригорском холме в сентябре.

He listened to his heart's fading quake,
to the clamorous squawk of rooks,
and mended those tatty roofs.
The river wound its sinuous course.
Snow fell. Cold weather lasted long.
And, acting out that civic resonance,
telephone wires moaned a song.

RUSSIAN DEPRESSION
For E. R.

All of Russia – right up from the trackless
road-to-nowhere median belt,
to the pole at the top of the Arctic
where the ice has started to melt,

inexhaustible Finnish drizzle,
Tauride lion stretched out in the heat
– it all found its place in your grizzled,
thinning-haired, dark-eyed head.

Blok and Khlebnikov crooned up your choler,
so they should carry the can.
The symptoms: hysteric, euphoric,
Moscow-in-January rant;

plus Petersburg garret distemper
in June, when nothing makes sense;
and wondrous Trigórskoe September –
equilibrium, reached only once.

В ПУСТОМ ЗАЛЕ

«Не отставайте», – нам сказали,
но мы отстали и одни
вдруг оказались в этом зале
с огромным зеркалом в тени.

На гобелене от Перикла
остался выцветший овал,
и рыхлый бархат слишком рыхло
на низком троне истлевал.

Сверкнули тусклые аканты
и корешки потёртых книг,
когда случайный луч закатный
в окно под потолком проник.

В нём золотая пыль дрожала
и он то вспыхивал, то гас,
но зеркало не отражало
ни света этого, ни нас.

IN THE EMPTY ROOM

'Don't fall behind', we had been told;
but we still did, and there we were –
suddenly in that room, alone
with a mirror, huge and shadowy.

A tapestry, once Pericles,
a faded oval now, no more;
a squat throne, velvet crumbling into dust
in all too dusty-velvet mode.

Murky acanthus glinted, and
the scuffed spines of a library;
a chance ray of the setting sun
poked through a window up on high.

There was a gleam of gold-dust motes,
that trembled in its lambent glow;
the mirror, though, sent nothing out –
no light above, no us below.

II
Из книги
КАК Я СКАЗАЛ (2005)

ЗАМЫВАНИЕ КРОВИ. УТОПЛЕНИЕ ТОПОРА

Замывание крови. Утопление топора.
Округление глаз на вопросы. «Где вы были вчера с полвторого
до полпятого?» – «Я? Уходил со двора,
был в трактире Ромашкина, спросите хоть полового».

Впрочем, это из книжек допотопной поры
про святых и студентов. Теперь забывают
рядом с трупом пустые бутылки и топоры,
на допросах мычат, да и кровь теперь не замывают.

НОВОСЕЛЬЕ

Сегодня ночью во сне
вы показали мне
вашу большую новую
квартиру. Через столовую,
где собранием стульев заведовал
стол, где я посоветовал
передвинуть рояль к окну,
мы прошли в гостиную,
а потом через залу пустынную
в спальню. Но почему одну?
И тотчас планировщик сна
показал: вот ещё одна
и ещё, спален было много,
много тёмных комнат для сна.

II
from
AS I SAID (2005)

THE BLOOD WASHED OFF. THE AXE DUMPED IN THE RIVER

The blood washed off. The axe dumped in the river.
Round-eyed replies: 'Where were you yesterday
half one to half four?' 'Me? Went out, and over
to Romashkin's inn – you ask the waiter, he can say'.

All that, though, comes from antediluvian novels
concerning saints and students. What they do now is
abandon axe and empty bottles by the body, mumble
when questioned, not bother washing off the blood.

THE NEW ABODE

In last night's dream
you two showed me round
your spacious new apartment.
First the dining room, with
table chairing a committee
of chairs, and I suggested
moving the piano nearer the window;
then the sitting room;
then an empty hallway; and then
the bedroom. Why only the one?
The planner of dreams
immediately pointed to one more,
and then yet more – there were many indeed,
many dark rooms for sleeping / dreaming.

Сегодня ночью во сне
вы друг друга почти что не
ненавидели, как в коммуналке,
свалке хлама, сортирной вонялке,
где вы прожили тридцать лет
при плакатах: «Гасите свет!»,
«Уходя выключайте свет!».
Слава богу, тут этого нет.

«Только вот, – вы твердили, – беда,
тут не будет метро никогда,
чтоб добраться, нужен десяток
ожиданий и пересадок,
руки книзу тянущих сумок,
скуки, всматривания в сумрак,
молчаливой ночной толчеи…»

Эти жалобы были ничьи,
чьи-то общие, мол, прописаться
очень трудно, но лучше мне
уходить, не остаться во сне,
просыпаться.

И, когда я в последний раз
оглянулся на дом ваш, гас
в окнах свет. Там гасили свет.
Выключали – и капитально
новый дом погружался во тьму.
В общем знаю я, почему
он враждебно глядел мне вслед.
Но ещё почему-то печально.

In last night's dream
the two of you almost didn't hate
each other, the way it was in that communal
dump, bog-standard stinkhole,
where for thirty years you lived
beneath signs saying TURN THE LIGHTS OFF!,
and LIGHTS OFF WHEN YOU LEAVE!
None of that here, thank God.

'The only trouble is,' I heard you say,
'the underground will never reach this far;
to get to here you have to wait and change
a dozen times at least,
arms weighed down with shopping bags,
then there's the boredom, the staring into the gloom,
the nightly crush when people don't converse...'

These strictures were anonymous,
seemingly shared, telling me that to move in here
would be very difficult, it'd be for the best
if I left, got out of the dream,
woke up, in fact.

And when I looked back for the last time
at this building of yours, the lights
in the windows were going out. Being switched off.
As they went out, your new abode,
all of a piece, faded into the gloom.
I have a fairly good idea why
it saw me off with hostile mien.
But there was something sad to it as well.

ОПЯТЬ НЕЛЕТНАЯ ПОГОДА

Вороний кар не только палиндром,
он сам карциноген. Распухла туча,
метастизирует. Кепчонку нахлобуча,
оставив за спиной аэродром,
куда теперь? Податься на вокзал?
Остаться и напиться в ресторане?
Как я сказал. Как кто-то там сказал
в стихах. Как было сказано заране.
Ведь я уже когда-то написал
о том, как дождь над полем нависал,
о тяжком сне пилота-выпивохи.
В другой стране, в совсем другой эпохе.
  ...

А может, ничего? Закрыть глаза
и к алтарю приткнуться аки агнец?
Вороны прячутся. Врывается гроза,
и подтверждают черный их диагноз.

ПАМЯТИ ПОЛЯРНИКА

О подлом бегстве ездовых собак,
о картах лгущих, о подошвах съеденных,
затерянная в *нрзб* сведеньях,
на нас глядит с последнего листа
овалом обведенная два раза
отчетливо-бессмысленная фраза:
«Альдебаран — слеза, а не звезда».

Такое написать на широте
0°, где тризну правит полюс!
Где, обеззвученный, вмерз в льдину санный полоз.
Где звезды замерзают в бороде.

GROUNDED AGAIN

The cawing crows evoke a darker 'c' –
cawcinogenic. And that cloud is swollen,
metastasizing. Cram your cap down lower,
abandon this old airfield – time to flee,
but where? Perhaps the station would be best.
Maybe stay there and tank up in the buffet.
It's as I said. Or anyway, said someone,
and in a poem. Before, somebody else.
I was the one, though, it was I who wrote
about the rain lowering above the field,
about the piss-arse pilot fast asleep.
Another country, and an age ago.
   ...

Perhaps do nothing? Should I shield my sight
and meekly as the lamb cleave to the altar?
The crows are cowering. Soon a storm will rattle,
and prove their blackest diagnosis right.

IN MEMORY OF A POLAR EXPLORER

Entries: the huskies did a bunk, the cowards;
the maps told lies; chewing on leather soles.
Forsaken among indecipherable words,
from the last page a phrase stares out at us.
A double oval ring sets it apart,
clear and precise but all the same absurd:
'Aldebaran's a tear and not a star.'

Imagine writing that at latitude
0° – the pole and naught besides!
It's where on stuck-fast sliders stands the silenced sled.
Where stars can fall into your beard, and turn to ice.

ПРОЗРАЧНЫЙ ДОМ

Наверное, налогов не платили,
и оттого прозрачен был насквозь
дом, где детей без счету наплодили,
цветов, собак и кошек развелось.

Но, видимо, пришел за недоимкой –
инспектор ли, посланец ли небес,
и мир внутри сперва оделся дымкой,
потом и вовсе из виду исчез.

Не видно ни застолий, ни объятий,
лишь изредка мелькают у окна
он (все унылее), она (чудаковатей),
он (тяжелей), (бесплотнее) она.

А может быть, счета не поднимались,
бог-громобой не посылал орла,
так – дети выросли, соседи поменялись,
кот убежал, собака умерла.

Теперь там тихо. Свет горит в прихожей.
На окнах шторы спущены на треть.
И мимо я иду себе, прохожий,
и мне туда не хочется смотреть.

**В ПОХОРОННОМ ДОМУ РАСШУШУКАЛАСЬ
ЖИЗНЬ-ВЫДВИЖЕНКА**

В похоронном дому расшушукалась жизнь-выдвиженка,
и как много ее –
с кучей мертвых цветов Черномырдин, с ТВ Евтушенко,
с Брайтонбича бабьё,

THE SEE-THROUGH HOUSE

Most like, the people hadn't paid their rates bill,
and that's why you could see straight through that house,
where children multiplied *ad infinitum*,
and so did flowers, and so did cats and dogs.

Then, someone must have come for what was owing –
an inspector, or an emissary from heaven;
at first, the world inside was misted over,
and then it vanished; there was nothing left.

Once in a while, you'd see flit past a window
(no table visible inside, nor bed);
him (heavier) or her (more incorporeal),
him (growing gloomier) or her (more odd).

Perhaps, though, there had been no final invoice,
no eagle sent down by a thundering god:
the kids grew up, and left; the neighbours ditto,
the cats ran off or died; so did the dogs.

It's quiet now. A light burns in the passage.
The blinds are one-third down all through the day.
And when I find I can't help walking past there,
I want to turn my eyes the other way.

THE FUNERAL PARLOUR'S ABUZZ WITH LIFE RISEN UP FROM THE RANKS

The funeral parlour's abuzz with life risen up from the ranks,
and more than a little:
Chernomyrdin with bunch of dead blooms, Yevtushenko fresh
      from a telecast,
Brighton Beach biddies,

и треножники камер, как тонкие ноги карамор,
налетевших на свет, и толпа,
положившая глаз на аристократический мрамор
желтоватого лба.

Словно пес потерявшийся, ветерок переменный,
вместо палки и мячика, разыгравшись, несет
запашок конопляного масла из китайской пельменной,
теплый вздох океана,
пар кофейный
к похоронному дому и от.

С.Д.

Я видал: как шахтер из забоя,
выбирался С.Д. из запоя,
выпив чертову норму стаканов,
как титан пятилетки Стаханов.
Вся прожженная адом рубаха,
и лицо почернело от страха.

Ну а трезвым, отмытым и чистым,
был педантом он, аккуратистом,
мыл горячей водой посуду,
подбирал соринки повсюду.
На столе идеальный порядок.
Стиль опрятен. Синтаксис краток.

Помню ровно-отчетливый бисер
его мелко-придирчивых писем.
Я обид не держал на зануду.
Он ведь знал, что в любую минуту
может вновь полететь, задыхаясь,
в мерзкий мрак, в отвратительный хаос.

and camera tripods like lean-legged mosquito marauders
that swarm towards the light. The crowd
casts an eye on the aristocratic marble
of that yellowish brow.

The shifting breeze, like a dog playing games with its owner,
is retrieving – not a ball or a stick, but odours:
whiff of sesame oil from a Chinese take-out,
the ocean's warm exhalation,
coffee vapour,
wafting them up to the funeral parlour and away.

S. D.

I've seen him emerge from oblivion,
like a miner out of the pithead,
after downing Lord knows how much over
the odds, a champ like Stakhanov.
Shirt singed by the fires of Hades,
and black in the face with horror.

But cleaned up, laundered, and sober,
a pedant he was, a fusspot –
washing dishes in good hot water,
mopping up the last little dust-mote.
The desk in apple-pie order.
Style and syntax clipped and sorted.

Those nit-picking letters, neatly
notated in tiny penpricks.
I didn't resent his needling.
For he knew that at any instant
he could plunge back down again, gagging,
to dark filth and revolting chaos.

Бедный Д.! Он хотел быть готовым,
оттого и порядок, которым
одержим был, имея в виду,
что, возможно, другого раза
нет, не вылезешь на свет из лаза,
захлебнешься кровью в аду.

    4 марта 2002г.

ИЗ БУНИНА
Нине

Прилетят грачи, улетят грачи,
ну а крест чугунный торчи, торчи,
предъявляй сей местности пасмурной
тихий свет фотографии паспортной.

Каждый легкий вздох – это легкий грех.
Наступает ночь – одна на всех.
Гладит мягкая звездная лапища
бездыханную землю кладбища.

    23-24 марта 2002, Oxford, Ohio

ОТРЫВОК

Лёг спать в июне – просыпаюсь в январе.
Не узнаю узоров на ковре
и за окном
безжизненный пейзаж мне незнаком.

Poor old D! He had to be ready –
here's what fuelled his rage for order –
he could never forget that maybe
the next time he might not be able
from the pit up to daylight to haul,
but would choke on his own blood in Hell.

    4 March 2002

OUT OF BUNIN
    for Nina

The rooks fly in and then fly out again;
this cast-iron cross, though, has to stand on guard,
presenting to this sombre plot of ground
the wan light of its passport photograph.

Each little sigh becomes a little sin.
The night's the same for all when it sets in.
A great big starry paw stroking the earth
of this graveyard, an earth that has no breath.

    23-24 March 2002, Oxford, Ohio

FRAGMENT

I went to bed in June, woke up again in Jan.
I can't decipher my own rug's design;
completely strange,
the lifeless scene beyond my window pane.

Литва ли, Закарпатье? Тишина
едва ли не враждой напряжена.
Какой-то зверь,
одетый человеком, входит в дверь.

Он черноглаз, до синевы побрит,
его язык, скрипучий, как санскрит,
мне незнаком,
как сосны, снег и тучи за окном.

Он, что ли, мне родня –
                            из неучтённых дядь?
Какую-то тетрадь мне норовит отдать,
я не беру, отдёргиваю руки.

Мне непонятны эти письмена,
но среди них я различаю имена
давно утраченного друга и подруги...

    7 апреля 2002

ПИРС ИСПАРИЛСЯ

Серый линкор отражен в синеве.
Парочки мирно воркуют себе,
гетеро и гомо,
и, как всегда у любой воды,
старый мудак на конце уды.
Тут мы как дома.

Доски повыщерблены. Линкор
на вечном приколе, в нем кулинар-
ная школа.

Lithuan- / Transcarpath-ia? No sound,
which makes the enmity feel more profound.
An unknown beast
comes through the door, dressed as a human being.

His eyes are black, his chin close-shaven blue,
his speech like Sanskrit, grating-rude,
completely strange,
like the pines, and snow, and clouds beyond my window pane.

Is this a relative I didn't know I had?
He's trying to thrust a notebook in my hand,
but I withdraw.

The writing in it is mysterious,
except two names: a man and woman I adored
long long ago, and lost.

7 April 2002

THE PIER THAT DISAPPEARED

A grey warship reflected in dark blue.
Couples who calmly bill and coo,
both hetero and homo;
plus what by any water you always find:
an old geezer at the end of his line.
This is where we felt at home.

The planking had seen better days. The warship
permanently docked, refashioned
as a catering school.

Плещутся волны. Смех поварят.
Баржи уходят за поворот
плавно и скоро.

То-то сюда мы ходили вдвоем,
друг мой, влюбленный в любой водоем,
я — тоже вроде.
Было да сплыло, исчезло, прошло.
Что вы там плещете, волны, назло?
Что вы там врете?

Было да сплыло, на то и вода.
Зря вот я трезвым приплелся сюда,
зря не напился.
То, что «сейчас» — это было «потом».
Тупо гляжу на железобетон.
Нет больше пирса.

ПОД СТАРОСТЬ ЗАБЫВАЮТ ИМЕНА

Под старость забывают имена,
стараясь в разговоре, как на мины,
не наступать на имя, и нема
вселенная, где бродят анонимы.

Мир не безумен — просто безымян,
как этот город N, где Ваш покорный
NN глядит в квадрат окошка чёрный
и видит: поднимается туман.

The waves lap. The cub cooks laugh.
Disappearing round the curve, barges plough
swift and smooth.

This is where we used to come, he and I.
My friend who adored water of any kind,
as I do too – well, sort of.
Now, all that has been and gone, disappeared, passed on.
Why do the lapping waves taunt me so?
Why do they tell tall stories?

To be and to go; that's what water is for.
To come here sober was no good at all –
I should have got pie-eyed.
What is 'here and now' was 'later' then.
So I stare dully at a concrete skeleton.
The pier has disappeared.

AS YOU GET ON, YOU CAN'T REMEMBER NAMES

As you get on, you can't remember names.
You try to tiptoe round these personnel mines
in conversation; but it's deathly mute,
this universe where the anonymous meet.

Nameless rather than senseless is this world.
Just like the town of X, and that is where
XX your obedient servant now observes
the mist rising beyond his black pane's square.

ГОРОД ЖИВЕТ, РАЗРАСТАЕТСЯ, СТРОИТСЯ

Город живет, разрастается, строится.
Здесь было небо, а нынче кирпич и стекло.
Знать, и тебе, здоровому, не поздоровится,
хватишься времени – нет его, истекло.

Выйдешь под утро в ванную с мутными зенками,
кран повернешь – оттуда хлынет поток
воплей, проклятий, угроз, а в зеркале
страшно оскалится огненноокий пророк.

СЕЙЧАС

1

Кот лежит на газете,
взглядом зелен и хмур,
в аккурат на портрете
Marianne Moore.

Нежива поэтесса,
чей портрет под котом.
У кота интереса
нет к тому, что потом.

Кот следит за синицей,
снег стряхнувшей с куста,
я – за этой страницей,
чтоб была не пуста.

THIS CITY'S ALIVE, BUILDING UPWARD AND OUTWARD

This city's alive, building upward and outward.
Brick and glass where once there was sky.
You too are a healthy thing, but health will be wounded;
by the time you think of it, time will run out and go by.

Into the bathroom, bleary-eyed of a morning;
you'll turn the tap on, hear the bursting stream seethe
with howls, curses, and threats, while in the mirror
a fiery-eyed prophet bares terrifying teeth.

RIGHT NOW

1

My cat's lying on a newspaper,
green-eyed and grim,
precisely covering a portrait
of Moore, Marianne.

She's dead, that lady poet
whose picture's under my cat.
And my cat has no interest
in what happens after that.

My cat has his eye on a bluetit
shaking snow from a branch;
and mine's on this white paper –
I wish it weren't so blank.

2

Снег не засыплется (ибо не пишется)
черной черникой.
Только не пыжиться! Только не пыжиться!
Чижик, чирикай!

На поле боя повалены воины,
на поле боли.
Только на воле бы! Только на воле бы!
Только б на воле!

Вспомнишь ли прошлое, зыбкое крошево,
где уж там пенье!
Тихо посвистывай, зябко взъерошивай
серые перья.

3

За окнами такой анабиоз,
такая там под минус тридцать стылость,
что яблоня столетняя небось
жалеет, что на свете загостилась.

Грозится крыша ледяным копьем.
Безвременный – день не в зачет, а в вычет.
Кот делится со мной своим теплом.
Мы кофе пьем. Один из нас мурлычет.

2

This snow won't get spattered (I'm blocked)
with black bilberry.
Mustn't get puffed up! Mustn't get puffed up!
Sing, little birdie!

Fallen warriors strew the field of battle,
the field of agony.
Must be free! Only when free!
If only free!

Can you remember the past, you fragile mite?
What song was there!
Whistle quietly, shudder, and fluff up your
grey feathers.

3

Outside it's anabiosis to such a degree –
to the minus thirty coolth –
that I bet our centurion apple tree
rues the day it sprang from earth.

An icy spear menaces from the eaves.
This day's out of time, one less instead of one more.
My cat's sharing his warmth with me.
We drink our coffee. One of us purrs.

III
Из книги
SISYPHUS REDUX (2000)

ИЮНЬ 1972 ГОДА

Тлели кнуты, плавились пряники.
Толковища наши стали тишать.
Горели в округе леса и торфяники.
Нечем стало дышать.

Жару объясняли протуберанцами,
происками ЦРУ из озоновых дыр,
а интеллигенция – засранцами
типа Брежнева и др.

Из вокзала плацентой из роженицы
с копейками, слипшимися во рту кошелька,
брели туда, где на месте мороженицы
сладкая лужица молока.

Что делать в стране, покинутой гением?
Вдавливаться с обрубком толпы
в красный трамвай, где по сидениям
ползут клопы.

Активность солнца. Пассивность нации.
Клопов мутации. Мусора
в серых мундирах прилипли к рации.
Период стагнации. Жара.

III
from
SISYPHUS REDUX (2000)

JUNE 1972

Sticks cooling to embers, carrots downgrated.
Our mob-scene get-togethers dying the death.
In the countryside, forest and peat conflagration.
Nothing to breathe.

People said the heat was from sunflares
and CIA dirty tricks with ozone holes;
intellectuals said it was from bumfluff
like Brezhnev & co.

Placenta-like, people plopping out of the station,
kopeck coins stuck in purse-mouth gunk,
then wandering on to where ice-cream ladies
had left a sweet pool of milk.

What to do in a country whose genius has departed?
Along with the stump of the crowd, elbow
your way into one of those red tramcars
with seats where bugs crawl.

Activity of sun. Passivity of nation.
Mutating bugs. And coppers in their grey
uniforms glued to their radio.
Period of stagnation. Heatwave.

ПОЧЕРК ДОСТОЕВСКОГО

С детских лет отличался от прочих
Достоевского бешеный почерк –
бился, дёргался, брызгался, пёр
за поля. Посмотрите-ка письма
с обличеньем цезаропапизма,
нигилизма, еврейских афёр,
англичан, кредиторов, поляков –
частокол восклицательных знаков!!!
Не чернила, а чернозём,
а под почвой, в подпочвенной черни
запятых извиваются черви
и как будто бы пена на всём.

Как заметил со вздохом графолог,
нагулявший немецкий жирок,
книги рвутся и падают с полок,
оттого что уж слишком широк
этот почерк больной, allzu russisch...

Ну, а что тут поделать – не сузишь.

РЕФОРМАТОР

Вроде как Моисей из пустыни,
вывел он прихожан из латыни,
рассадил по немецким скамьям.
Чёрным кофе и булочкой сдобной
отдавал его ямб пятистопный,
зарифмованный ямб, ямб как ямб.

Представляете – маленький Лютер.
Рядом с мальчиком Vater und Mutter.

DOSTOEVSKY'S HANDWRITING

It was different ever since boyhood,
Dostoevsky's frenzied hand: rabid,
writhing, twitching, spattering, elbowing
over margins. Those letters, denouncing
caesaropapism, choking on
nihilism, Jewish jiggery-pokery,
the English, his creditors, Poles –
exclamation stockades of points!!!
Not black ink, but black humus,
and beneath, in under-earth gloom,
the wormy wriggle of commas,
and everything smeared with scum.

A graphologist once said, grimly,
(lard-layered from German good living)
that his books explode off the shelf,
for they're all too lacking in self-
control – *allzu russisch,* that sick writing.

What to do, though? No way to confine it.

THE REFORMER

Like Moses out of the wasteland,
he led his flock out of Latin
and put them to German schooling.
His iambic pentameter was redolent
of black coffee and rich bread rolls,
and it rhymed, the way it should do.

Picture the little Luther.
Flanked by his *Vater* and *Mutter.*

Где-то сонно гнусавит прелат.
Но цветной вдруг врывается ветер,
загорается в раме Санкт-Петер,
сердоликом одежды горят,

аметистом, рубином, смарагдом.
Благовонием рая и смрадом
преисподней бросает в дрожь.
Индульгенцией не опасёшься.
Дуй на кофе – а то обожжёшься.
Хлеб преломишь – иголку найдёшь.

СТОП-КАДР

Где это было? В каком-то немецком – как его там? –
                                                                                     городке.
Скверный прохожий в костюмчике мерзком с пуделем на
                                                                                     поводке,
он обратился ко мне на неместном, т.е. на моём, языке.

Так предлагают украденный кодак, девку на вечер, порно.
Тоже находка! Подобных находок в уличной давке полно.
Шёпот вонючий был жарок и гадок, я отвернулся бы, но

я вообще не люблю продолженья, знанья, что будет потом.
Вот и кивнул на его предложенье. Пудель подёргал хвостом.

Pastor nasalling soporific sermon.
Then boom! a wind blows, iridescent,
framed St. Peter is incandescent,
his raiment ablaze with cornelian,

amethyst, ruby, smaragd.
Convulsions from the fragrance
of heaven, the fug from nether regions.
No refuge in any indulgence.
Blow on your coffee, lest it scald you.
Break bread, and you'll find a needle.

FREEZE-FRAME

Where did it happen? In Germany, small town – what in the
                                                                               world was its name?
Poodle on leash, something nasty came strolling toward me,
                                                                                a vile-suited man,
who then addressed me in a language not local. And it turned
                                                                              out to be mine.

That's how they pitch you a contraband camera, porn, or a
                                                                      one-night-stand broad.
Thanks, but no thanks. Every crowd on the pavements
                                                                     offers such deals. And that bad-
breath hiss was hot and horrendous, and maybe, I should have
                                                                    turned away, but

I've never liked it when things keep unrolling, don't care to
                                                                       wait for an end.
Poodle's tail twitched when to master's proposal I gave a nod
                                                                          of assent.

*Чёрной спиралью застыло круженье ласточек в небе пустом,
в неизменяемом небе закатном звук колокольный застыл,
замерли стрелки часов.*

      А за кадром – солнце пускалось в распыл,
стрелки часов по обычным законам двигались. Колокол бил.

Жизнь продолжала гулять, горлопанить, крыть, не терять куражу,
далью манить, алкоголем дурманить, счёт предъявлять к платежу.
Всё, что сберёг я, – открытку на память. Что потерял –
не скажу.

*High in the void of the sky a black whorl of swallows that
                              hung there suspend-
-ed, in that static dusk sky all the grinding bells had abandoned
                                                    their toil,
hands of the clocks all stood still.*

Meanwhile wider, outside the frame, the sun broiled,
hands on the clocks all went on with their gliding. Only a single
                                                      bell tolled.

Life's pandemonium continued, it bickered, cursed, then went
                                                    on anyway,
summoned afar, stupefied with strong liquor, menaced with bills
                                                    to be paid.
All that I kept was a postcard reliquary. But what I lost, I won't say.

IV
Из книги
ПОСЛЕСЛОВИЕ (1998)

ПОСЛЕСЛОВИЕ

Послесловие

С января на сорок дней
мир бедней.

Тычась в мертвые сосцы
то ль волчицы, то ль овцы,

сорок дней сосут твое
из него отсутствие.

Агнец стих. Не воет волк.
Мир умолк.

Не скребет по древу мышь.
Всюду тишь.

Воронья стая на дворе.
Чернила стынут на пере.

Снег на мраморе стола.
Бумага белая бела.

  8 марта 1996

* * *

IV
from
AFTERWORD (1998)

AFTERWORD

AFTERWORD

Since January, by forty days
the world is poorer.

Butting the lifeless dug
of she-wolf or of ewe,

those forty days suck out
your absence from it.

Lamb bleats no more; and wolf has ceased to howl.
The world has fallen silent.

No mouse scratches across the wood.
Quiet everywhere.

A flock of crows outside.
Ink clotting on the nib.

Snow on tabletop marble.
White paper white.

    8 March 1996

    * * *

Холод (1921-1996)

Я знаю: он родился в сороковом году; он помнить не может. И все-таки, читая его, я каждый раз думаю: нет, он помнит, он сквозь мглу смертей и рождений помнит Петербург двадцать первого года, тысяча девятьсот двадцать первого лета Господня, тот Петербург, где мы Блока хоронили, где мы Гумилева не могли похоронить.
В.Вейдле

Веки и губы смыкаются в лад.
Вот он – за дверью,
и уступают голос и взгляд
место забвенью.

Ртуть застывает, как страж на посту –
нету развода.
Как выясняется, пустоту
терпит природа,

ибо того, что оставлено тлеть
под глиноземом,
ни мемуарам не запечатлеть,
ни хромосомам.

Кабы не скрипки, кабы не всхлип
виолончели,
мы бы совсем оскотинились, мы б
осволочели...

Ветер куражится, точно блатной,
тучи мучнисты.
С визгом накручивают одной
ручкой чекисты

страшные мерзлые грузовики
и патефоны,

Cold (1921-1996)

I'm well aware that he was born in 1940 and therefore he can't possibly remember. But all the same, when I read him I always think that he does remember – through the fog of deaths and births he remembers the Petersburg of 'twenty-one, the year of Our Lord 1921, the Petersburg where we buried Blok and were unable to bury Gumilev.

Vladimir Veidle

Eyelids and lips close in concert.
He's left the room,
and voice and vision cede
place to oblivion.

The mercury stiffens like a sentry
whose relief won't come.
Nature, as it turns out,
adores a vacuum,

for that which is left to decay
in the clay soil
cannot be put on record, in diary
or chromosome.

Without that violin, without the sobbing cadence
of that cello, we
would have become either cattle
or swine...

The wind whistles up its courage, like a gangster,
whipping the mealy clouds.
And the Cheka death squad cranks, one-handed,
a crowd

of lorry engines, sluggish from the frost,
and wind-up gramophones,

чтоб заглушать винтовок хлопки
и плач Персефоны.

    март 1996-23 декабря 1997

    * * *

Коринфских колонн Петербурга
прически размякли от щелока,
сплетаются с дымным, дремотным,
длинным, косым дождем.
Как под ножом хирурга
от ошибки анестезиолога,
под капитальным ремонтом
умирает дом.

Русского неба буренка
опять ни мычит, ни телится,
но красным-красны и массовы
праздники большевиков.
Идет на парад оборонка.
Грохочут братья камазовы,
и по-за ними стелется
выхлопной смердяков.

    4 апреля 1996, Eugene

    * * *

Включил ТВ – взрывают домик.
Раскрылся сразу он, как томик,
и пламя бедную тетрадь
пошло терзать.
Оно с проворностью куницы

so as to muffle the rifle shots
and Persephone's moans.

   March 1996-23 December 1997

   * * *

The chevelure of Petersburg columns –
corinthian softened by alkali –
interweave with the sleepy, smoky,
long-drawn-out, slanting rain.
Under its major remodelling,
as if by surgeon's scalpel
after anaesthetist's blunder,
a building passes away.

The Russian sky, that old brown cow,
still chews its cud, won't come clean,
but red as red and mass as mass
the Bolshevik show goes on.
Row upon row parade the warheads;
the brothers Kamaz rumble and scream,
spreading behind them the gas
and stink of exhaust smerdyakov.

   4 April 1996, Eugene

   * * *

I turned on the TV and saw a house blown up.
It fell open like a volume dropped;
flames victimized
its pitiful quires.
Nimble as a pine marten, ranging

вмиг обежало все страницы,
хватало пищу со стола
и раскаляло зеркала.
Какая даль в них отражалась?
Какое горе обнажалось?
Какую жизнь сожрала гарь —
роман? стихи? словарь? букварь?
Какой был алфавит в рассказе —
наш? узелки арабской вязи?
иврит? латинская печать?
Когда горит, не разобрать.

30 апреля 1996, Eugene

* * *

На кладбище, где мы с тобой валялись,
разглядывая, как из ничего
полуденные облака ваялись,
тяжеловесно, пышно, кучево,

там жил какой-то звук, лишенный тела,
то ль музыка, то ль птичье пить-пить-пить,
и в воздухе дрожала и блестела
почти несуществующая нить.

Что это было? Шепот бересклета?
Или шуршало меж еловых лап
индейское, вернее бабье, лето?
А то ли только лепет этих баб —

той с мерой, той прядущей, но не ткущей,
той с ножницами? То ли болтовня

over all the pages,
from the table seizing meat,
making mirrors melt.
What distant scene did they reflect?
What grief did they detect?
What kind of life was gobbled by the searing heat –
novel? poem? dictionary? ABC?
What alphabet did the story use –
ours? Knotted Arabic curlicues?
Hebrew? Roman? No way to know
when something's going up in smoke.

30 April 1996, Eugene

* * *

The graveyard where we spent some idle moments
watching the ways the mid-day clouds sculpted
themselves from nothing, heavy-loaded,
luxuriantly, keeping edges scalloped –

that place was home to a sound inchoate:
music perhaps, or '*drink-drink-drink*' birdcall,
and in the air, trembling and glowing,
hung a thread, almost ethereal.

Now what was that? The hawthorn whisper?
Or was it squaw Indian summer worming
between the paws of the spruces?
Or was it only the babble of those old women,

one with a measure, one spinning but declining
to weave, the third with shears? Maybe the Connecticut

реки Коннектикут, в Атлантику текущей,
и вздох травы: «Не забывай меня».

5 мая 1996, Eugene

* * *

Где воздух «розоват от черепицы»,
где львы крылаты, между тем как птицы
предпочитают по брусчатке пьяццы,
как немцы иль японцы, выступать;
где кошки могут плавать, стены плакать,
где солнце, золота с утра наляпать
успев и окунув в лагуну локоть
луча, решает, что пора купать, –
ты там застрял, остался, растворился,
перед кофейней в кресле развалился
и затянулся, замер, раздвоился,
уплыл колечком дыма, и – вообще
поди поймай, когда ты там повсюду –
то звонко тронешь чайную посуду
церквей, то ветром пробежишь по саду,
невозвращенец, человек в плаще,
зека в побеге, выход в зазеркалье
нашел – пускай хватаются за колья, –
исчез на перекрестке параллелей,
не оставляя на воде следа,
там обернулся ты буксиром утлым,
туч перламутром над каналом мутным,
кофейным запахом воскресным утром,
где воскресенье завтра и всегда.

9 мая 1996, Eugene

* * *

gossiping towards the Atlantic,
and the grass sighing 'Forget me not'.

    5 May 1996, Eugene

* * *

Where the air itself is 'pink-tinged from the pantiles',
and lions have wings; while birds don't care to fly,
instead displaying on the cobbled piazzas
like the Japanese and German tourist tide;
where cats can swim and walls can shed a teardrop;
where the sun takes time to limn itself in gold
in the morning, sends a ray to dip an elbow
and check the temperature of the lagoon –
that's where you fetched up, stayed, assimilated,
took a deep drag in armchair café lounge,
relaxed, grew still, then turned into a double,
wafted away like a wisp of smoke, and now
just try to guess, when you are omnipresent:
sometimes you make the teaset of a church
ring out, or else you zephyr through a garden –
the non-returner, man in mackintosh,
the GULag escapee who found an exit
through to behind the mirror; then, effaced,
you left us at the crosspoint of the mapmarks,
leaving upon the water not a trace –
you might go by as fragile little tugboat,
nacre of cloud above a dull canal,
coffee aroma on a Sunday morning,
to rise again next day, for good and all.

    9 May 1996, Eugene

* * *

Последняя в этом печальном году
попалась мыслишка, как мышка коту...

Обратно на свой залезаю шесток,
ее отпускаю бежать на восток,
но где ей осилить Атлантику! –
силенок не хватит, талантику.

Мой лемминг! Смертельная тяжесть воды
навалит – придется солененько,
и луч одинокой сверхновой звезды
протянется к ней, как соломинка.

    1-5 февраля 1997

    * * *

Архипелаг
Янгфельдтам

Дабы лазурь перекрещивал кадмий,
ветер гуляет стервец стервецом,
свет облакам выделяя – блокадный
тусклый урезанный рацион.

Все мы собою в таком околотке
изображаем смешную беду
подлой – нет, бедной! – советской подлодки,
в шхерах застрявшей у всех на виду.

Что ж, с днем рождения! – примем лекарство
горького шнапса – на миг исцелит,
ибо вокруг нас – небесное царство,
хвойная память, вечный гранит.

I cat-nabbed a wee, sleekit, cowrin... idea,
the last of this doleful departed year...

Now I clamber back to my know-your-place,
releasing the beastie to skitter off east;
but for lasting out the Atlantic
he's lacking both training and talent.

My poor little lemming! A salty death-weight
will flood over him. He'll be in for a fight.
But the beam from a lone supernova star
will reach down towards him, like a straw.

1-5 February 1997

* * *

The Swedish Islands
For the Jangfeldts

In order that cadmium delete azure,
as bold as a buzzard the wind ranges,
apportioning colour to clouds – a wizened
wartime siege ration.

Every one of us in this situation
configures the comical debacle
of the despicable – no, pitiful! – Soviet Navy
sub stuck on the skerries in full view of all.

So, happy birthday, then! We'll take the medicine
of bitter schnapps, it'll put us right for a minute,
for round about us is the heavenly kingdom:
pine-needle memory, eternal granite.

Берег с морщиной, прорезанной льдиной,
так и застыл со времен ледника,
сплошь обрастая мхом, как щетиной
мертвая обрастает щека.

24 мая 1997, Стокгольм

* * *

Римский полдень

Три пчелы все не вытащат ног из щита Барберини,
или, как срифмовал бы ты, в Риме бери не
хочу вечных символов, эмблем, аллегорий и др.
В вечной памяти нет прорех, пробелов и дыр.

Оседлал облака, что приснятся тебе и Ламарку,
император, себя воплотивший в коренастую арку,
Тит, который ходил молотить наших пращуров в Иудее.
С раскоряченным всадником сходны мраморные затеи.

Так на облачном белом коне триумфатор въезжает на Форум,
чтобы сняться с туристами. А другой император, с которым
у тебя больше общего, в окруженье пятнистого дога,
утешает нас тем, что жизнь не имеет итога.

Это я просто так, чтобы время убить, для порядку.
Вот невзрачная бабочка совершает промашку
и мешает писать, совершая посадку на эту тетрадку,
принимая ее за большую ромашку.

9 июня 1997, Foro Romano

* * *

The wrinkled shore, scored by icebergs,
has been frozen in time since the ice receded,
growing its even carpet of moss, like stubble
sprouting on the cheeks of a dead man.

    24 May 1997, Stockholm

    * * *

Roman Mid-Day

Those three bees simply can't unstick their feet from the Barberini
shield – or, as you would have rhymed it: in Rome I can't bear to be reading
those eternal symbols, emblems, allegories, et al's.
In eternal memory there are no tears, gaps, or holes.

He saddled the clouds that you and Lamarck see in your dreams,
that emperor who embodied himself in a thick-set arch –
Titus, who went forth to smite our forbears in Judaea.
These marble whims remind us of that legs-akimbo horseman.

Thus on a white steed of cloud the man of the hour rides into the Forum,
to have his picture taken with the tourists. But another emperor, with whom
you have more in common, circled by a dalmatian,
consoles us by saying that life has no conclusion.

I'm saying all this for no reason, to kill time, for form's sake.
A dull little butterfly is doing something it shouldn't,
not helping me write by landing on my notebook,
taking it for a huge camomile.

    9 June 1997, Foro Romano

    * * *

Pietà

Мертвый мрамор,
обвисший с отверделых
от горя мраморных колен.

Мраморный зрачок
не реагирует на свет, но вспышка
за вспышкой все продолжают пробовать – а вдруг! –
японцы, немцы…

13 июня 1997, Рим

ПАМЯТИ МИХАИЛА КРАСИЛЬНИКОВА

Песок балтийских дюн, отмытый добела,
еще хранит твой след, немного косолапый.
Усталая душа! спасибо, что была,
подай оттуда знак – блесни, дождем покапай.

Ну, как там, в будущем, дружище футурист,
в конце женитьб, и служб, и пересыльных тюрем?
Давай там встретимся. Ты только повторись.
Я тоже повторюсь. Мы выпьем, мы покурим.

Ведь твой прохладный рай на Латвию похож,
но только выше – за закатными лучами.
Там, руки за спину, ты в облаке бредешь,
привратник вслед бредет и брякает ключами.

18 сентября 1997

PIETÀ

Mortal marble,
drooping from grief-hardened
marble knees.

Marble pupil
does not react to the light, but there's one flash
after another as they keep on trying – maybe next time! –
those Japanese and Germans...

    13 June 1997, Rome

IN MEMORY OF MIKHAIL KRASILNIKOV

The Baltic dunes, their sand washed out to white,
still bear your footprints, just a little twine-toed.
You weary soul, I thank you for your life;
signal to me from there, with rain or lightning.

My futurist friend, how's things in time to come,
with marriages and jobs and jails all weathered?
I'll see you there. You have a second run,
and so will I. We'll raise a glass together.

Your chilly heaven's like Latvia, after all,
beyond the sunset, though, and also higher.
Hands behind back, on clouds you take your walk;
clinking his keys, a warder tracks behind you.

    18 September 1997

ВТОРОЕ РОЖДЕНИЕ

Я книгу нашел! Там в какой-то столовой,
прохладной, как ухо врача,
возилось чудовище тучи лиловой,
вспухая, вздыхая, ворча,

там сколько могли от больного скрывали,
что пульса и музыки нет.
Настройщик порылся, порылся в рояле
и вытащил черный предмет –

и вдруг окатило всех мокрой сиренью,
и вспыхнул на маковках крест,
и новые власти прочли населенью
такой золотой манифест,

что в даль протянулись растений волокна
и птицей запрыгала близь,
и все отраженные зеркалом окна
на книжной странице зажглись.

Я И СТАРАЯ ДАМА (Норвич, 1987-1997)

Жертва козней собеса, маразма, невроза,
в сальном ватнике цвета «пыльная роза»,
с рюкзаком за спиной, полным грязного хлама,
в знойный полдень проходит под окном моим дама.
Так задумчиво, что и жара ей не в тягость.

Десять лет (т.е. *лет* – с июня по август)
после утренних лекций под окном ровно в полдень
наблюдал я цветочек этот Господень.
Будь я Зощенкой, Шварцем или Олешей,
я б сумел прочитать в этой всаднице пешей,

A SECOND BIRTH

I once found a book, in a dining room
as clammy as a doctor's ear,
where a monstrous purple cloud loomed –
growing, gasping, and grouchy –

and where they did anything but let the patient know
he had no pulse, no music.
Then along came the tuner, rummaged inside the piano,
extracted something dark,

and in a trice everyone was drenched in lilac,
cupola crosses were all aglow;
a new authority proclaimed to the populace
a golden manifesto:

that filaments of growing plants extend into the far,
while like a bird, the near hop-hops around.
And all the windows in the mirror caught fire
on the pages of that book I'd found.

ME AND THE OLD LADY (Norwich, 1987-1997)

Ground down by social security, senility, neurosis,
wearing a greasy, 'dusty rose' parka
and a backpack stuffed with filthy clobber,
in the midday heat this lady walks by my window.
So deep in thought, the heat to her's no burden.

Ten years of summers, June to August,
after morning lectures, at mid-day precisely
I would observe this flower of Creation.
If I were Zoshchenko, Shvarts, or Olesha,
I might discern in this pedestrian equestrienne,

в этом ангеле, бледном от серого пота,
сладкозвучный оракул: «Нищета есть свобода».

Только где те писатели? где тот оракул?
где то чтение знаков? где тот кот, что наплакал
веры? Нету. Писатели тихо скончались.
Вместе с ними религия, психоанализ,
символизм и вермонтская летняя школа.
Лишь осталась картина, на манер протокола –
занесенная в память: «Я и старая дама».

Обрамляет картину белая рама
от упавшего в прошлое чужого окна.

И другая картина пока не видна.

6 января 1998

СЕРДЦЕБИЕНИЕ
Меж топких берегов извилистой реки...
           Полонский

Где леса верхушки глядят осовело,
           когда опускаешь весло,
где двигалось плавно, но что-то заело,
           застряло, ко дну приросло
                  (сквозь сосны горячее солнце сочилось,
                  торчали лучи наискось,
                  но смерклось, исчезло, знать, что-то случилось,
                  печальное что-то стряслось),
           его сквозь себя пропускают колхозы,
           пустые поля и дома
                  уткнуться, где гнутся над омутом лозы,
                         где в омуте время и тьма.

1988

in this angel dusted with grey perspiration,
a mellifluous oracle uttering 'Poverty is Freedom'.

Except where are those writers? Where that oracle?
Where that reading of omens? Where the hide and
hair of faith? All gone. The writers quietly departed.
And along with them went religion, psychoanalysis,
symbolism – and the Summer School at Norwich.
All that's left is a scene etched in my memory
like an indictment: 'Me and the Old Lady'.

Around this scene is the white border of someone
else's window, one that's dropped into oblivion.

And, as yet, no different scene can be discerned.

6 January 1998

HEARTBEAT
Tween swampy banks of winding river...
                                         POLONSKY

A place where the treetops look on entranced
        as you dip in your blade;
smoothly gliding along – but then something snags,
        sticks, takes root in the bed
        (through the pines seeps burning sunshine,
        rays poking aslant,
        but then it fades and goes in; there must be something,
        something surely sad);
        the collective farms, the empty fields and houses
        allow this sadness through,
        so's to dig in where over the pool bend osiers,
        and in the depths are time and gloom.

1988

V
Из книги
НОВЫЕ СВЕДЕНИЯ О КАРЛЕ И КЛАРЕ
(1996)

НЕТ

Вы русский? Нет, я вирус СПИДа,
как чашка жизнь моя разбита,
я пьянь на выходных ролях,
я просто вырос в тех краях.

Вы Лосев? Нет, скорее Лифшиц,
мудак, влюблявшийся в отличниц,
в очаровательных зануд
с чернильным пятнышком вот тут.

Вы человек? Нет, я осколок,
голландской печки черепок –
запруда, мельница, проселок...
а что там дальше, знает Бог.

БЕЗ НАЗВАНИЯ

Родной мой город безымян,
всегда висит над ним туман
в цвет молока снятого.
Назвать стесняются уста
трижды предавшего Христа
и все-таки святого.

Как называется страна?
Дались вам эти имена!

V
from
**NEW INFORMATION CONCERNING CARL AND CLARA
(1996)**

NOT

'You're Russian?' 'No, virus-ian AIDS,
life's teacup smashed to little bits,
piss-artist playing walk-on parts;
I grew up over there, that's it.'

'You're Loseff?' 'No, Lifshits am I,
the prat who fell for girls with brains,
and yawnmakers with charming ways
who bore an inkstain you know where.'

'You're human?' 'No, I am a shard,
a chunk chipped off a Holland stove,
with pond, and mill, and country road,
and where it leads, God only knows.'

UNTITLED

My native city has no name;
the fog that shrouds it stays the same –
it's skimmed-milk white all over.
Lips hesitate to speak out loud
of him who thrice denied his Lord,
yet counts among the holy.

And what's my country called, you say.
Why the obsession with these names?

Я из страны, товарищ,
где нет дорог, ведущих в Рим,
где в небе дым нерастворим
и где снежок нетающ.

ВЕТХАЯ ОСЕНЬ

Отросток Авраама, Исаака и Иакова
осенью всматривается во всякий куст.
Только не из всякого Б-г глядит и не на всякого:
вот и слышится лишь шелест, треск, хруст.

Конь ли в ольшанике аль медведь в малиннике?
Шорох полоза? Стрекот беличий? Крик ворон?
Или аленький, серенький, в общем маленький, но длинненький
пришепетывает в фаллический микрофон?

Осень. Обсыпается знаковость, а заповедь
оголяется. С перекрестка душа пошла вразброд:
направо Авраамович, назад Исаакович,
налево Иаковлевич, а я – вперед.

В АЛЬБОМ О.
Про любовь мне сладкий голос пел…
Лермонтов

То ль звезда со звездой разговор держала,
то ль в асфальте кварцит норовил блеснуть...
Вижу, в розовой рубашке вышел Окуджава.
На дорогу. Один. На кремнистый путь.

– The land I come from, comrade,
is where no road can lead to Rome,
and where the sky is smoke and fume,
and snow stays frozen solid.

OLD TESTAMENT AUTUMN

In autumn, the sprig of Abraham, Isaac, and Jacob
carefully inspects every kind of bush.
But G-d looks out not from all of them, nor at everyone;
instead, there are sounds: rustle, crackle, crunch.

Antler in alder or bruin in bramble?
Swishing sleigh-runner, strident squirrel, croaking crow?
Or is some little thing, scarlet, grey, small but long-backed
whispering into a phallic microphone?

Autumn. Signification sheds its leaves, and the country park
grows bare. At the fork, my soul goes different ways:
son of Abraham right, son of Isaac back,
son of Jacob left, and I go straight.

FOR O'S SCRAPBOOK
A sweet voice sang to me of love...
                    LERMONTOV

It could have been one star conversing with another,
or quartz in asphalt trying hard to glint...
I saw – wearing a pink shirt, out walked Okudzhava.
Onto the road. Alone. I saw. That 'path of flint'.

Тут бы романсам расцветать, рокотать балладам,
но торжественных и чудных мы не слышим нот.
Удивляется народ: что это с Булатом?
Не играет ни на чем, песен не поет.

Тишина бредет за ним по холмам Вермонта
и прекрасная жена, тень от тишины...
Белопарусный корабль выйдет из ремонта,
снова будут паруса музыкой полны.

Отблеск шума земли, отголосок света,
ходит-бродит один в тихой темноте.
Отражается луна в лысине поэта.
Отзывается струна неизвестно где.

ЗАБЫТЫЕ ДЕРЕВНИ

В российских чащобах им нету числа,
все только пути не найдем –
мосты обвалились, метель занесла,
тропу завалил бурелом.

Там пашут в апреле, там в августе жнут,
там в шапке не сядут за стол,
спокойно второго пришествия ждут,
поклонятся, кто б ни пришел –

урядник на тройке, архангел с трубой,
прохожий в немецком пальто.
Там лечат болезни водой и травой.
Там не помирает никто.

Along with him should come the ring of song, the roil of ballad,
but no notes do we hear – moody, miraculous.
People have been amazed: what's happened to Bulat?
Lately he plays no instrument and sings no songs.

Silence follows his steps around the Vermont hillocks,
so does that handsome wife, his silent shade...
The bark refitted will emerge from drydock,
music once more will stiffen that white sail.

Reflector of earth's sound, and to its light responder,
into the quiet dark this wanderer walks alone.
The moon strikes a refraction from the poet's tonsure.
A string sounds in response; where, is unknown.

FORGOTTEN VILLAGES

In the Russian wilds there's too many to count;
but no path to them can be found:
by flood and storm the bridges are cut,
and weeds have barraged the road.

There in April they plough, in August they reap,
they bare their heads to sit down;
they patiently wait for Christ to appear,
but whoever appears, they bow –

to troika-borne constable, archangel with horn,
to strange-coated passerby.
They doctor their ailments with water and herb,
and none of them ever die.

Их на зиму в сон погружает Господь,
в снега укрывает до стрех –
ни прорубь поправить, ни дров поколоть,
ни санок, ни игр, ни потех.

Покой на полатях вкушают тела,
а души веселые сны.
В овчинах запуталось столько тепла,
что хватит до самой весны.

ДЖЕНТРИФИКАЦИЯ
Светлане Ельницкой

Река валяет дурака
и бьет баклуши.
Электростанция разрушена. Река
грохочет вроде ткацкого станка,
чуть-чуть поглуше.

Огромная квартира. Виден
сквозь бывшее фабричное окно
осенний парк, реки бурливый сбитень,
а далее кирпично и красно
от сукновален и шерстобитен.

Здесь прежде шерсть прялась,
сукно валялось,
река впрягалась в дело, распрямясь,
прибавочная стоимость бралась
и прибавлялась.

Она накоплена. Пора иметь
дуб выскобленный, кирпич оттертый,
стекло отмытое, надраенную медь,

God vouchsafes them sleep the winter through,
and the snow piles up roof-high;
no ice-hole vigil, no chopping of wood,
no sleighrides, no games, no delight.

Their bodies find peace as they lie on their shelves,
and their souls dream dreams full of cheer.
So much warmth has lodged in their rough sheepskins,
it'll last until spring is here.

GENTRIFICATION
    for Svetlana Yelnitskaya

These days, the river only fools about,
idling its time away.
The power plant's in ruins. The water, though,
still roars like the machines it drove,
with stifled wave.

A huge apartment. Through
what was a factory window, view
the autumn park, the river's molten-honey seethe,
and further off, the brick-red hue
of fulling mills that used to bash and beat.

In this place woollen thread was spun,
and woven bolts stood stacked around,
the river buckled down in regulated run,
and surplus value grasped and grubbed,
so it accrued.

Enough accumulated. Now it's time
for sanded oak, squared-up scrubbed tile,
for burnished brass and polished pane,

и слушать музыку, и чувствовать аортой,
что скоро смерть.

Как только нас тоска последняя прошьет,
век девятнадцатый вернется
и реку вновь впряжет,
закат окно фабричное прожжет,
и на щеках рабочего народца

взойдет заря туберкулеза,
и заскулит ошпаренный щенок,
и запоют станки многоголосо,
и заснует челнок,
и застучат колеса.

ПАРИЖСКАЯ НОТА

Он вынул вино из портфеля,
наполнил стакан в тишине.
Над крышами башня Эйфеля
торчала в открытом окне.

Заката багровая кромка
кропила отлив жестяной.
«… vraiment ça finit mal», – громко
вдруг кто-то сказал за стеной.

Такая случайная фраза
в такие печальные дни
бросает на кухню, где газа
довольно – лишь кран крутани.

piped music. Artery, though, and vein
murmur that death is nigh.

And when the ennui endgame leaves us broke,
the nineteenth century will come again,
and cinch the river back into its yoke.
The mounting sun will light the factory gate,
upon the visage of the labouring folk

will rise the glow from the consumptive lung,
the scalded factory dog will moan,
the looms break into polyphonic song,
the shuttle snap back with its to-and-fro,
and wheels will claque along.

THE PARISIAN NOTE

He took out the wine from his briefcase,
and silently poured for himself.
In the window, over the roofscape
towered the Tour Eiffel.

The crimson selvedge of sunset
flecked the zinc-surfaced sill;
'…vraiment ça finit mal', a voice said,
loud through the party wall.

A chance phrase, overheard, like this one,
during days of such tristesse,
and you well might make for the kitchen,
where it's easy to turn on the gas.

ПОДРАЖАНИЕ

Как ты там смертника ни прихорашивай,
осенью он одинок.
Бьется на ленте солдатской оранжевой
жалкий его орденок.
За гимнастерку ее беззащитную
жалко осину в лесу.
Что-то чужую я струнку пощипываю,
что-то чужое несу.
Ах, подражание! Вы не припомните,
это откуда, с кого?
А отражение дерева в омуте –
тоже, считай, воровство?
А отражение есть подражание,
в мрак погруженье ветвей.
Так подражает осине дрожание
красной аорты моей.

С ГРЕХОМ ПОПОЛАМ (15 ИЮНЯ 1925 ГОДА)

... и мимо базара, где вниз головой
из рук у татар
выскальзывал бьющийся, мокрый, живой
блестящий товар.

Тяжелая рыба лежала, дыша,
и грек, сухожил,
мгновенным, блестящим движеньем ножа
ее потрошил.

И день разгорался с грехом пополам,
и стал он палящ.
Курортная шатия белых панам
тащилась на пляж.

IMITATION

Tart up death-facing man all you can,
in autumn he stands alone.
His pathetic gong (he served in the ranks)
swings on its orange ribbon.
For its no-camouflage tunic in the woods,
I pity the aspen tree.
This is some alien string I've touched,
alien vestment for me.
Imitation, of course! But can you recall,
where it's from, of whom?
Reflected tree in a deep forest pool:
is that sort of stealing, too?
But reflection must also be imitation,
immersion of boughs into dark.
Just as the naked aspen's vibration
is imitated by my red heart.

THERE BUT FOR... (15 JUNE 1925)

… and on past the bazaar. Headlong slither
down from Tartar hands
of flailing, glittering, wet, alive
merchandise –

fat fish that lay there choking
until a wiry Greek,
with an instant, glittering strike,
knifed open their guts.

The day warmed up – only just, firstly –
then started to scorch.
The white-panama leisure crowd filed
down to the beach.

И первый уже пузырился и зрел
в жиру чебурек,
и первый уже с вожделеньем смотрел
на жир человек.

Потом она долго сидела одна
в приемной врача.
И кожа дивана была холодна,
ее — горяча,

клеенка — блестяща, боль — тонко-остра,
мгновенен — туман.
Был врач из евреев, из русских сестра.
Толпа из армян,

из турок, фотографов, непманш-мамаш,
папашек, шпаны.
Загар бронзовел из рубашек-апаш,
белели штаны.

Толкали, глазели, хватали рукой,
орали: «Постой!
Эй, девушка, слушай, красивый такой,
такой молодой!»

Толчками из памяти нехотя, но
день вышел, тяжел,
и в Черное море на черное дно
без всплеска ушел.

Как вата склубилась вечерняя мгла
и сдвинулась с гор,
но тонко закатная кровь протекла
струей на Босфор,

In its own grease bubbled to doneness
the first cheburek;
grease gazed at with longing eyes
by the first-come chap.

And she sat there a long time, lonesome
in the doctor's anteroom.
The hide on the sofa was cold,
but hers burned,

the lino gleaming, subtle-sharp the hurting,
then instant mist.
The doctor Jewish, Russian the nurse.
The crowd was Armenians,

Turks, photographers, Mrs-spiv mummies,
old queens, and layabouts.
Sunburn gleaming through buttonless
shirts and bleached pants.

Pushing and staring and finger-pointing,
pleading 'Hold on, pleeze!
Hey, yong lady – so preetty,
so yong she ees!'

In unwilling gobs leaving memory – but still surely –
the heavy day inched
down into the black depths of the Black Sea,
making no splash.

Like cotton wool, the evening gloom mopped up,
moved off the mountainous shore,
then subtly the sunset blood seeped
into the Bosphorus,

на хищную Яффу, на дымный Пирей,
на злачный Марсель.
Блестящих созвездий и мокрых морей
неслась карусель.

На гнутом дельфине – с волны на волну –
сквозь мрак и луну,
невидимый мальчик дул в раковину,
дул в раковину.

and on to rapacious Jaffa, smoky Pireus,
and fatted Marseilles.
Glittering constellations and wet seas
whirled like a carousel.

Riding a round-backed dolphin billow to billow
by moon's silver and grey,
into his conch there blew and blew
a phantom boy.

VI
Из книги
ТАЙНЫЙ СОВЕТНИК
(1987)

АПРЕЛЬ 1950

Вижу: вот он идет с медосмотра
с дифтерийной прививкой в плече,
и ребенка жидовская морда
розовеет и жмурится в нежном апрельском луче.

Как известно, в периоды Ирода дети
улыбаются сами себе.
Поднимается жар. Зажигается свет в кабинете.
Корифей дифтерита в сапогах зашагал по судьбе.

Он уже выбирает из русского списка комочки еврейских фамилий.
Он в ночи-сортировочной составляет товарные поезда.
Но зачем прививается славянская тяжесть крылий?
Ах, зачем нам ширококрылость тогда?

Как слезу не сглотнуть в этом первом полете,
если сверху не то что виднее – родней
трубы, крыши да в воробьином помете
триумфальные спины коней.

ТУАЛЕТ

На подзеркальнике мерцают цацки –
нецке, цепочки, выцинанки, кольца, яйца,
снесенные под пасху Фаберже,
а возле дымно–розовых флаконов
венецианских, датской голубой

VI
from
PRIVY COUNCILLOR
(1987)

APRIL 1950

I can see him coming back from the clinic,
diphtheria jab sprouting from shoulder,
Jew-boy face rosy, eyes crinkled
against the soft sunshine of an April day.

When Herods are in power, of course,
babies can't keep a smile off their face.
It's hotting up. The light goes on in the office.
The prince of pockmarks plants his jackboots on our fate.

Picking out clots of Jewish names from his Russian list.
Coupling up trains in his dead-of-night marshalling yard.
So why be injected with weighty Slavonic wings?
For the likes of us, what's the point of a span so broad?

So tears must be choked back on this maiden flight;
after all, overhead – homely to sense but harder to see –
there are chimneys and roofs, and sparrow-lime
on the cruppers of those triumphal steeds.

TOILETTE

Knick-knacks glimmered there beneath the mirror:
netsuke, chainlets, cutouts, rings, those eggs
Fabergé used to lay at Eastertime,
some smoky-pink Venetian vials set
to flank a sky-blue Danish piglet, and

свиньи вся в инкрустации шкатулка
персидская, хранилище квитанций
за газ, за телефон, за свет, рецептов
на остродефицитный стрептоцид,
на красном дереве в прожогах от щипцов
пороша розовато—жирной пудры,
а золотой цилиндрик ярко-красным
пятном отметил голубой конверт,
где вместо марки черный-черный штамп:
ПРОВЕРЕНО ВОЕННОЙ ЦЕНЗУРОЙ –
ЙОРУЗНЕЦ ЙОННЕОВ ОНЕРЕВОРП,
поскольку розовое, голубое,
персидско-датское, щипцы и стрептоцид,
все это пробиралось в зазеркалье,
где и мерцал в венецианском дыме,
беззвучно квохча, Фаберже – он снес
цепочку, или нецке, иль кольцо?
рецепт на телефон иль веронал?
иль это галицийская безделка?
         . . . .
         . . . .

над этим миром жило не лицо,
а черная бумажная тарелка,
играющая «Интернационал».

В ГРОССБУХ

Я по природе из тетерь.
Не перечесть моих потерь –
стихов, приятелей, ключей,
в дымину пропитых ночей;

an inlaid Persian casket made to serve
as a receptacle to store receipts,
(gas, telephone, electric light) and also
prescriptions for a scarce bacterial ointment,
and on mahogany scorched by curling-irons
a dusting of some powder, greasy-pink,
a little golden cylinder reflecting
a bright red spot on a blue envelope
without a stamp, instead, a jet-black imprint:
FIELD CENSORSHIP: INSPECTED AND APPROVED –
DEVORPPA DNA DETCEPSNI :PIHSROSNEC DLEIF,
reversed because those colours, pink and blue,
the Persian-Danish stuff, the irons, the ointment,
was infiltrating back behind the mirror,
where glimmered Fabergé in Venice fog, –
silently clucking, which was it that he laid
– necklace, or netsuke, or perhaps a ring?
The prescription for the phone or for the ointment?
Or was it all cheap trinkets from Galicia?
....
....

over this world there hovered, not a visage,
but a black platter fashioned out of paper,
that used to play 'The International'.

LEDGER ENTRY

By nature I'm a careless sod.
Who knows how many things I've lost –
the lines of verse, the friends, the keys,
the nights in alcoholic haze;

то телефонный разговор
похитит полчаса, как вор,
то дети как-то без затей
вдруг выросли – и нет детей.
Я давеча, страшась сумы,
у дара своего взаймы
решил спросить. Какой удар!
Мне отказал мой дивный дар.
И ты, Брут! Так сказать, et tu!
И ты показываешь тыл?
А Муза Памяти? Тю-тю,
ее давно и след простыл.
А Муза Разума? Она
сама в себе отражена
и не дает, зараза, в долг.
Мой лучший друг, Тамбовский Волк,
мотает серой головой:
я, дескать, сам пустой, хоть вой.
Давно уж Музы ни гу-гу,
давно уже сидит в мозгу
бухгалтер, а точней – чекист.
Командует взять чистый лист,
число поставить, месяц, год
и записать: в расход.

ДЕКАБРЬСКИЕ ДИКИЕ СНЫ

Декабрьские дикие сны.
Ночи с особым режимом.
Не я, а рельефная карта страны
лежит на матрасе пружинном.

a conversation on the phone
and half an hour is stolen, gone;
somehow my kids all by themselves
have suddenly grown up and left.
The other day I was running low
and asked my gift to make a loan
to keep me solvent. Well, take that!
My wondrous gift turned me down flat.
Brutus, you too! (*et tu!* i.e.),
how could *you* turn your back on me?
The Muse of Memory? O no,
she disappeared long ago.
The Muse of Reason? Not a chance,
she only steps to her own dance,
gives nothing in advance, the whore.
My bosom pal, the Tambov Wolf,
shakes its grey head as it says nay:
nothing to give, howl as you may.
It's ages since the Muses sighed,
my brain has long been occupied
by an accountant; nay – a spook.
He bids me take an empty book,
set down the hour, the day, the month,
the year, and enter: written off.

DECEMBER DREAMS COME IN A CRAZY RUSH

December dreams come in a crazy rush, in
nights on strict regime.
And no longer I, but a relief map of Russia
stretches over the mattress springs.

Из мелкой подушки мой питер торчит —
и надо же этак разлечься! —
то чешется вильнюс, то киев бурчит,
то крым подбивает развлечься.

Но слева болит, там, где кама течет,
в холодной пермяцкой подмышке,
где медленно капает время в зачет
несчастному Мейлаху Мишке.

РАЗБУЖЕН НЕОЖИДАННОЙ ТИШИНОЙ

Разбужен неожиданной тишиной
белым внезапным с неба даяньем.
Отвергаю с негодованьем,
нет, с равнодушием, ужас ночной.

Вертикально вниз среди разветвлений
разных растений, растущих в саду,
сходит к нам Бог атмосферных явлений,
чтобы развеять нашу беду.

My piter protrudes from flat pillowland –
how could my pose be so awkward?
First my vilnius starts itching, my kiev then bitches,
then my crimea wants to go walkies.

My left flank hurts, where the kama plays
via my chilly uralian armpit,
and slowly, slowly counts off the days
being served by poor Misha Meilakh.

AWAKENED BY AN UNEXPECTED SILENCE

Awakened by an unexpected silence,
a sudden gift from heaven, white as white,
with indignation I reject – should say
indifference – the horrors of the night.

Vertically downwards, through the matted
growing things that crowd my garden plot,
here comes the God of atmospheric matters,
in order to disperse our parlous lot.

VII
Из книги
ЧУДЕСНЫЙ ДЕСАНТ
(1985)

МЕСТОИМЕНИЯ

Предательство, которое в крови.
Предать себя, предать свой глаз и палец,
предательство распутников и пьяниц,
но от иного, Боже, сохрани.

Вот мы лежим. Нам плохо. Мы больной.
Душа живет под форточкой отдельно.
Под нами не обычная постель, но
тюфяк-тухляк, больничный перегной.

Чем я, больной, так неприятен мне,
так это тем, что он такой неряха:
на морде пятна супа, пятна страха
и пятна черт чего на простыне.

Еще толчками что-то в нас течет,
когда лежим с озябшими ногами,
и все, что мы за жизнь свою налгали,
теперь нам предъявляет длинный счет.

Но странно и свободно ты живешь
под форточкой, где ветка, снег и птица,
следя, как умирает эта ложь,
как больно ей и как она боится.

VII
from
THE MIRACULOUS RAID
(1985)

PRONOUNS

There's treachery that's carried in the blood:
betrayal of oneself, one's eye and finger;
there's treachery of debauchee and drinker –
but from a different kind save me, O Lord.

We're lying here. We're feeling bad. We're ill.
Up by the window lives our soul, quite separate.
Beneath us there's no ordinary bed, but
a putrid palliasse in a hospital.

The patient I displeases me for that
he keeps himself in such filthy disorder;
there's soupstains on his gob, and stains of terror
and something else, God knows what, on the sheet.

There's still another thing pulsating through our veins,
while we lie there with feet growing more chilly:
it's every lying act we have committed
coming to call, demanding settlements.

How strange, though, and how free you live up there
with tree branch, snow, and bird outside the window,
watching the way that falsehood's life is winding
down, so full of pain and full of fear.

ТРАМВАЙ

На Обводном канале,
где я детство отбыл,
мы жестянку гоняли –
называлось: футбол.
Этот звук жестяной
мне охоту отбил
к коллективной игре
под кирпичной стеной.

Блещут мутные перлы
треть столетья назад.
Извержения спермы
в протяженный мазут.
Как мешочки медуз,
по каналу ползут
эти лузы любви,
упустившие груз.

Нитяной пуповиной
в Обводный канал,
нефтяною лавиной –
на фабричный сигнал,
предрассветный гудок
подгонял, подгонял
каждый сон, каждый взгляд,
каждый чаю глоток.

Позабыт, позамучен
с молодых юных лет.
Вон в траве, замазучен,
мой трамвайный билет,
ни поднять, ни поддать
(сырость, кости болят).
Цифры: тройка, семерка.
Остальных не видать.

THE TRAM

By the Bypass Canal
I served time as a kid.
We would chase a tin can –
it was soccer, we said.
That clank and that clink
exorcised my esteem
for games played in teams
next to walls built of brick.

Thirty years have elapsed,
but those clouded pearls gleam,
ejaculate sperm
in that oily black stream.
Sort of jellyfish vials
sliding down that canal,
go the scumbags of love
that have slopped out their load.

An umbilical cord
to the Bypass Canal
was the grease-lava coil
of the factory's call:
that siren pre-dawn
gathered insistently
every glance, every dream,
every mouthful of tea.

Forlorn in the grass
from those youthyears of mine
lies my old tramcar pass,
crumpled, grubby, begrimed.
I can't take it or leave
(aching bones from the damp).
Serial number: 3, 7…
The rest I can't grasp.

Этот стих меня тащит,
как набитый трамвай,
под дождем дребезжащий
над пожухлой травой;
надо мне выходить
было раньше строфой;
ничего, не беда,
посижу взаперти
со счастливым билетом
во взмокшей горсти.

ЖИВУ В АМЕРИКЕ ОТ СКУКИ

Живу в Америке от скуки
и притворяюсь не собой,
произношу дурные звуки —
то гортовой, то носовой,
то языком их приминаю,
то за зубами затворю,
а сам того не понимаю,
чего студентам говорю.
А мог бы выглядеть достойно,
и разговорчив, и толков,
со мной коньяк по кличке «Дойна»
Глазков бы пил или Целков,
и, рюмочку приподнимая,
прищурив отрешенный глаз,
я бы мычал, припоминая,
как это было в прошлый раз —
как в час удалой поздней встречи
за водкой мчались на вокзал.
Иных уж нет, а я далече
(как сзади кто-то там сказал).

This poem's hauled me away
like that tight-packed old tram,
thrumming under the rain,
over grass turned to brown.
Time to've got up and gone
a whole stanza ago –
though the harm isn't much;
I shall sneak a side seat,
lucky ticket I'll clutch
in a hand slick with sweat.

I'M LIVING IN THE STATES FROM BOREDOM

I'm living in the States from boredom,
pretending that I'm someone else,
pronouncing these unpleasant noises,
some in the throat, some through the nose,
some of them by my tongue extruded,
others locked in behind my teeth,
and nothing that I tell my students
makes any sense at all to me.
I could have been of worthy aspect,
with much to say that meant a lot,
partaking of a decent cognac,
Glazkov to share it, or Tselkov.
And as my arm would raise the snifter,
one slightly narrowed eye aloof,
I would recall with voice uplifted
what happened at our last set-to,
how we nipped out when shades were falling
for vodka from the station bar.
Some are no more, and I'm past calling
(as somebody once said back thar').

ТЕМ И ПРЕКРАСНЫ ЭТИ СНЫ

Тем и прекрасны эти сны
что все же доставляют почту
куда нельзя, в подвал, в подпочву,
в глубь глубины,

где червячки живут, сочась,
где прячут головы редиски,
где вы заключены сейчас
без права переписки.

Все вы, которые мертвы,
мои друзья, мои родные,
мои враги (пока живые),
ну, что же вы

смеетесь, как в немом кино.
Ведь нет тебя, ведь ты же умер,
так в чем же дело, что за юмор,
что так смешно?

Однажды, завершая сон,
я сделаю глубокий выдох
и вдруг увижу слово *выход* –
так вот где он!

Сырую соль с губы слизав,
я к вам пойду тропинкой зыбкой
и уж тогда проснусь с улыбкой,
а не в слезах.

THE SPLENDID THING ABOUT THESE DREAMS

The splendid thing about these dreams
is that they get your mail beyond
the bounds, to underground
deepest of deeps,

where worms live in their sleazy way,
radishes keep their heads well down,
where you're all incommunicado,
locked in your jail.

So you, the ones who've gone before,
who were my friends, my relatives,
enemies even, while alive –
why are you all

laughing, like in a silent film?
Each one of you has ceased to be,
so what's up, where's the comedy,
why all the fun?

One of these days, putting away
a dream, I'll heave a great big sigh,
and then I'll see the 'Exit' sign –
so *that's* the way!

I'll lick the raw salt from my mouth,
set off towards you down a fragile
path, then wake up with a smile
and weep no more.

ЗЕМНУЮ ЖИЗНЬ ПРОЙДЯ ДО СЕРЕДИНЫ

1

Земную жизнь пройдя до середины,
я был доставлен в длинный коридор.
В нелепом платье бледные мужчины

вели какой-то смутный разговор.
Стучали кости. Испускались газы,
и в воздухе подвешенный топор

угрюмо обрубал слова и фразы:
все ху да ху, да е мае, да бля –
печальны были грешников рассказы.

Один заметил, что за три рубля
сегодня ночью он кому-то вдует,
но некто, грудь мохнатую скобля,

ему сказал, что не рекомендует,
а третий, с искривленной головой,
воскликнул, чтоб окно закрыли – дует.

В ответ ему раздался гнусный вой,
развратный, негодующий, унылый,
но в грязных робах тут вошел конвой,

а я был унесен нечистой силой.
Наморща лобик, я лежал в углу.
Несло мочой, карболкой и могилой.

В меня втыкали толстую иглу,
Меня поили горечью полынной.
К холодному железному столу

потом меня доской прижали длинной,
и было мне дышать запрещено
во мраке этой комнаты пустынной.

HAVING TRAVERSED HALF MY THREE SCORE AND TEN

1

Having traversed half my three score and ten,
I was delivered to an endless corridor.
Wearing outlandish costumes, some pale men

debated, but I hadn't a clue what for.
Bones knocked together. Gases were released.
An axe somehow suspended in mid-air

grimly lopped off the ends of word and phrase,
so all I heard was fu and cu and chri –
pitiful indeed were these poor sinners' tales.

One of them said that later on that night
three rubles straight would guarantee he'd score,
another scratched his hairy chest and cried

he couldn't manage that stuff any more,
the third, who had a weird distorted head,
complained of draughts and said to shut the door.

In answer there came shrieking, full of dread,
indignant, but perverted and depraved.
An escort dressed in filthy smocks appeared

and, emissaries of hell, took me away.
I languished in a corner, with furrowed frown.
A stink of piss, carbolic, and the grave.

They took a needle thick as a tree bough
and shot my veins full of some bitter rheum.
And then they pressed me flat and down

to a metal table with an enormous spoon,
and told me I must not breathe in or out
within the darkness of this desolate room.

И хриплый голос произнес: «Кино».
В ответ визгливый: «Любоваться нечем».
А тот: «Возьми и сердце заодно».

А та: «Сейчас, сперва закончу печень».
И мой фосфоресцировал скелет,
обломан, обезличен, обесцвечен,

корявый остов тридцати трех лет.

2

От этого, должно быть, меж ресниц
такая образовывались линза,
что девушка дрожала в чей, и шприц,

как червячок, и рос и шевелился.
Вытягивалась кверху, как свеча,
и вниз катилась, горяча, больница.

(То, что коснулось левого плеча,
напоминало птицу или ветку,
толчок звезды, зачатие луча,

укол крыла, проклюнувшего клетку,
пославший самописку ЭКГ
и вкривь и вкось перекарябать сетку

миллиметровки.) Голос: «Эк его».
Другой в ответ: «Взгляни на пот ладоней».
Они звучали плохо, роково,

но, вместе с тем, все глуше, отдаленней,
уже и вовсе слышные едва,
не разберешь, чего они долдонят.

A hoarse voice: 'That's some movie, there's no doubt!'
A squeaky-voiced response: 'God, what a waste!'
Hoarse voice: 'Let's get the heart while we're about

it.' 'Hang about, I'll do the liver first'.
My skeleton had a phosphorescent glow,
disjointed, de-individualized, debased,

a bony scaffold, thirty-three years old.

2

Because of what had happened, no doubt, the fringe
formed by my lashes shaped a kind of lens
that made the sister tremble; the syringe

looked like a worm, one that stretched out and flexed.
And candle-like, the hospital towered up,
and then collapsed, demolished by the flames.

(By something my left shoulder-blade was dubbed
that seemed to be a bird or else a branch,
a winking star, a ray of light fresh-scrubbed,

a wingtip sticking through a cage's bars,
that then dispatched an autograph ECG,
scrawling across and up and down the chart

of the graph paper.) A voice came: 'In a state, he
is'. The response, 'His palms are soaking wet'.
The voices seemed resigned to fate's decree,

but got more and more hollow, further away,
so much that they could hardly now be heard,
I couldn't comprehend what it all meant.

Я возлетал. Кружилась голова.
Мелькали облака, неуследимы.
И я впервые обретал слова,

земную жизнь пройдя до середины.

3

Ты что же так забрался высоко,
Отец? Сияет имя на табличке:
«… в чьем ведении Земля, Вода и К°…»
И что еще? Не разберу без спички.
День изо дня. Да, да. День изо дня
Ты крошишь нам, а мы клюем, как птички.

Я знаю, что не стребуешь с меня
долгов (как я не вспомню ведь про трешку,
что занял друг), не бросишь, отгоня

пустого гостя. Просит на дорожку
хоть посошок… Вот черт! Куда ни кинь…
За эту бесконечную матрешку,

где в Царстве Сила, в Силе Слава…

СОНЕТ

Мне памятник поставлен в кирпиче,
с пометой воробьиной на плече
там, где канал не превращает в пряжу
свою кудель и где лицом к Пассажу

I'd taken wing. My head was in a whirl.
Clouds flashed past faster than I could attend.
And for the first time I was given the gift of words,

having traversed half my three score and ten.

3

Why have you made your way so high above,
O Father? The signboard glitters like a screen:
'...in whose dominion Earth, Water & Co...'

What else, what else? I need a match to see.
Day after day. Yes, yes. Day after day
you scatter, and like birds we come to feed.

I know thou wilt not ask me to repay
my debts (I don't remember when I lend
a friend three roubles), you will not drive away

the unfed guest. He's asking for assent,
one for the road... Curses! Wherever you look...
Beyond this damned matryoshka with no end

where Power is in the Kingdom, Glory in Power...

SONNET

It's built of brick, the monument to me,
and on its shoulders sparrows pay their fee,
by that place where the canal fails to spin out
the wool it's wound; the place where, faced about

сидит писатель с сахаром в моче
в саду при Александр Сергеиче,
и мне, глядящему на эту лажу,
дождь по щекам размазывает сажу.

Се не со всех боков оштукатурен
я там стою, пятиэтажный дурень,
я возвышаюсь там, кирпичный хрыч.

Вотще на броневик залез Ильич –
возносится превыше мой кирпич,
чем плешь его среди больниц и тюрем.

ПРОДЛЕННЫЙ ДЕНЬ
И ДРУГИЕ ВОСПОМИНАНИЯ
О ХОЛОДНОЙ ПОГОДЕ

*На острове, хранящем имена
увечных девочек из княжеского рода,
в те незабвенные для сердца времена
всегда стояла теплая погода.*

Нина Мохова

I

Я ясно вижу дачу и шиповник,
забор, калитку, ржавчину замка,
сатиновые складки шаровар,
за дерево хватаясь, суевер.
Я ясно вижу – злится самовар,
как царь или какой-то офицер,
еловых шишек скушавший полковник
в султане лиловатого дымка.
Так близко – только руку протяни.
Но зрелище порой невыносимо:

towards the Arcade, with sugar in his pee,
a writer sat in Pushkin Square we see;
and as I contemplate this sorry sight
the rain comes down and smears my cheeks with soot.

Behold, 'tis I – not altogether plastered –
there I do stand, five-storey silly bastard,
there in these bricks I rise, old grouch himself.

In vain did Lenin mount that armoured car:
my bricolage is higher than him by far,
bald pate girt round by hospital and jail.

**THE EXTENDED DAY,
AND OTHER MEMORIES
OF COLD WEATHER**
> *And on that island they preserved the names
> of maidens from the princely clan,
> from times my heart can not forget
> when winter never came.*
> николаю Mokhova

I

I see it clear: the dacha, the wild roses,
the wooden fence, the gate with rusted latch,
the shiny-wrinkled, baggy summer trousers;
I touch wood, superstitious as I am.
I see it clear: the samovar is fuming
like tsar or some high officer annoyed –
a colonel who's been fuelled up with fircones,
and shakoed by a plume of lilac smoke.
So near, hold out your hand and you can feel it,
but there's some sights you don't care to repeat:

еще одна позорная Цусима,
японский флаг вчерашней простыни.

А на крыльце красивый человек
пьет чай в гостях, не пробуя варенья,
и говорит слова: «Всечеловек...
Арийца возлюби... еврей еврея...
отсюда шаг один лишь, но куда?
до царства Божия? до адской диктатуры?»

Теперь опять зима и холода.
Оленей гонят хмурые каюры
в учебнике (стр. 23).
«Суп на плите, картошку сам свари».

Суп греется. Картошечка варится.
И опера по радио опять.
Я ясно слышу, что поют – арийцы,
но арии слова не разобрать.

II

Продленный день для стриженных голов
за частоколом двоек и колов,
там, за кордоном отнятых рогаток,
не так уж гадок.

Есть много средств, чтоб уберечь тепло
помимо ваты в окнах и замазки.
Неясно, как сквозь темное стекло,
я вижу путешествие указки
вниз, по маршруту перелетных птиц,
под взглядами лентяев и тупиц.
На юг, на юг, на юг, на юг, на юг.
Оно надежней, чем двойные рамы.

a second shameful battle of Tsushima –
the rising sun spread out on last night's sheet.

A handsome chap holds forth on the veranda,
a guest for tea, ignoring the preserves,
and speaking words like 'Universal manhood...
for Aryans respect... Jews to love Jews...
Which way to go? From here it's one small step –
God's kingdom or devil's dictatorship?'

And now it's back to winter cold. The reindeer
are being rounded up by grim-faced Lapps
in textbook fashion (see p. 23).
'Soup's on the stove-top, you can do the spuds'.

Soup on to warm. The spuds are boiling merry.
It's opera on the radio, no doubt.
I hear it clear: the singers are the Aryans,
the aria's words I simply can't make out.

II

Extended day for close-cropped little noggins
kept in by a stockade of failing scores,
but catapults can't cross the cordon, so things
for me could be considerably worse.

There's many ways of holding in the warmth
besides packing the window frames with mastic.
Dimly, as through a darkened pane, I watch
the teacher's pointer travel downwards, tracking
along the path of birds' migration route,
observed by dunderhead and lazybones.
South, to the south, it's always to the south.
This holds in heat better than double glazing.

Напрасно академия наук
нам вслед радиограммы,
«Я полагаю, доктор Ливингстон?»
В ответ счастливый стон.

Края, где календарь без января,
где прикрывают срам листочком рваным,
где существуют, обезъян варя,
рассовывая фиги по карманам.
Мы обруселых немцев имена
подарим этим островам счастливым,
засим вернемся в город над заливом —
есть карта полушарий у меня.

Вот желтый крейсер с мачтой золотой
посередине северной столицы.
В кают-компании трубочный застой.
Кругом висят портреты пустолицы.
То есть уже готовы для мальца
осанка, эполет под бакенбардом,
история побед над Бонапартом
в союзе с Нельсоном и дырка для лица.

Посвистывает боцман-троглодит.
На баке кок толкует с денщиками.
Со всех портретов на меня глядит
очкастый мальчик с толстыми щеками.

III

Евгений Шварц пугливым юморком
еще щекочет глотки и ладони,
а кто-то с гардеробным номерком
уже несется получить галоши.
И вот стоит, закутан до бровей,

The Academy of Sciences in vain pursuit
dispatching wireless cables after us.
And then it's 'Dr Livingstone, I presume?'
And in response, a groan of happiness.

Where January's absent from the diary,
shame-saving leaf covers the fount of grief,
stewed monkey meat provides the staple diet,
figs grow on trees, so no-one gives a fig.
We'll christen these happy islands, these we'll dub
with names of russified Germans, and thereafter
we'll sail back to the city on the gulf –
the hemispheres are in my schoolboy atlas.

A yellow-hulled and golden-masted cruiser
is beached within the northern capital.
Her wardroom solid pipe-smoking infusion.
There's blank-faced portraits hung on every wall.
I mean, all ready for the boy are martial
deportment, sideburn over shoulderboard,
the story of defeating Bonaparte
allied with Nelson, – instead of face, a hole.

The hard-man bosun pipes up with his whistle.
Stewards take orders from the galley cook.
From every portrait down at me is watching
a little specky boy with chubby cheeks.

III

Our palms and throats still tickly from applauding
a play by Shvarts in cringing-comic mode;
someone has been dispatched, clutching the token,
to get the galoshes from the garderobe.
Little me waiting, swaddled to the eyebrows,

ждет тройку у Михайловского замка,
в кармане никнет скомканный трофей —
конфетный фантик, белая программка.

Опущен занавес. Погашен свет.
Смыт грим. Повешены кудель и пакля
на гвоздик до вечернего спектакля.
В театре хорошо, когда нас нет.
Герой, в итоге победивший зло,
бредет в буфет, талончик отрывая.
А нам сегодня крупно повезло:
мы очень скоро дождались трамвая.

Вот красный надвигается дракон,
горят во лбу два разноцветных глаза.
И долго–долго, до проспекта Газа,
нас будет пережевывать вагон.

IV
И он, трепеща от любви и от близкой Смерти...
                                          В. Жуковский

Над озером, где можно утонуть,
вдоль по шоссе, где могут раскорежить,
под небом реактивных выкрутас
я увидал в телеге тряской лошадь
и понял, в травоядное вглядясь,
что это дело можно оттянуть.
Все было, как в краю моем родном,
где пахнет сеном и собаки лают,
где пьют за Русь и ловят карасей.
где Клавы с Николаями гуляют,
где у меня полным–полно друзей.
Особенно я вспомнил об одном.

for a troika by the Mikhailovsky House,
with crumpled trophy fading in the pocket –
the toffee-paper programme from the show.

The curtain's down. The lights have all been doused.
The greasepaint washed away. Oakum and horsehair
hung on their nails until the second house.
It's nice, a theatre with no audience.
After his last-act triumph over evil,
meal-ticketed hero makes for the buffet.
And for us too there is a fine finale –
our tram arrives almost without a wait.

A scarlet dragon coming on, right at us,
two different-coloured eyes burn at its brow.
And all the long long way to Prospekt Gaza
is peristalsis in the monster's bowel.

IV
The young man, all agog with love and fast-approaching Death...
ZHUKOVSKY

Above a lake in which one might well drown,
along a road where one might be knocked down,
beneath a sky of con-trail dash and dot
I saw a horse pulling a rickety cart,
and realised as I watched that herbivore
that these components made up something more.
This entire scene was like my native parts –
where hay is fragrant and the dogs do bark,
toasts raised to Russia, carp hooked on the line,
where Klava walks out with her Nikolai,
and where there are so many friends of mine.
One in particular sprang to my mind.

Неслыханный мороз стоял в Москве.
Мой друг был трезв, задумчив и с получки.
Он разделял купюры на две кучки.
Потом, подумав, брал с собою две.
Мы шли с ним в самый лучший ресторан,
куда нас недоверчиво впускали,
отыскивали лучший столик в зале,
и всякий сброд мгновенно прирастал.
К исходу пира тяжелел народ,
и только друг мой становился легок.
Тут выяснялось, что он дивный логик
и на себя все объяснить берет.
Он поднимался в свой немалый рост
средь стука вилок, кухонной вонищи
и говорил: «Друзья, мы снова нищи
и это будет наш прощальный тост.
Так выпьем же за стройный ход планет,
за Пушкина, за русских и евреев
и сообщением порадуем лакеев
о том, что смерти не было и нет».

V

... в «Костре» работал. В этом тусклом месте,
вдали от гонки и передовиц,
я встретил сто, а, может быть, и двести
прозрачных юношей, невзрачнейших девиц.
Простуженно протискиваясь в дверь,
они, не без нахального кокетства,
мне говорили: «Вот вам пара текстов».
Я в их глазах редактор был и зверь.
Прикрытые немыслимым рваньем,
они о тексте, как учил их Лотман,
судили как о чем-то очень плотном,
как о бетоне с арматурой в нем.

Even for Moscow, this frost was a hard one.
My friend was sober, pensive, flush with dough.
He split his banknotes into two big handfuls.
Reflected, then decided to take both.
We went to the top restaurant in the city,
they let us in, although they had their doubts;
we wheedled the best table, set up business,
and hangers-on immediately turned out.
Much gravitas was gained as platters emptied –
not by my friend, for he was growing light,
turning into a quite amazing mentor,
with plans to set the entire world to rights.
Stretching himself to his considerable measure,
to clashing forks, and also kitchen stink,
he said: 'Behold, my friends, once more we're beggars,
and this will be our final farewell drink!
Let's toast the planets on their constant way,
Pushkin, the Russians and their friends the Jews,
let's bring good news to all who stand and wait,
and tell them there's no death, and never was.'

v

... I worked on *Campfire*. In that dismal hole,
a long way from the ratrace and newsmakers,
I met a hundred – two, for all I know,
transparent youths and most uncomely maidens.
Down with a cold, they'd creep up to my desk,
and, with a touch of arrogant flirtation,
announce: 'I've brought along a couple of texts.'
An editor, to them I was like Satan.
Shielded behind their vast pretentiousness,
they talked about the text, as taught by Lotman,
as if it were an impenetrable mass,
a slab of concrete with an armature in.

Все это были рыбки на меху
бессмыслицы, помноженной на вялость,
но мне порою эту чепуху
и вправду напечатать удавалось.

Стоял мороз. В Таврическом саду
закат был желт, и снег под ним был розов.
О чем они болтали на ходу,
подслушивал недремлющий Морозов,
тот самый, Павлик, сотворивший зло.
С фанерного портрета пионера
от холода оттрескалась фанера,
но было им тепло.
                  И время шло.
И подходило первое число.
И секретарь выписывал червонец.
И время шло, ни с кем не церемонясь,
и всех оно по кочкам разнесло.
Те в лагерном бараке чифирят,
те в Бронксе с тараканами воюют,
те в психбольнице кычат и кукуют,
и с обшлага сгоняют чертенят.

   VI

Мой самый лучший друг и полувраг
не прибирает никогда постели.
Ого! за разговором просидели
мы целый день. В окошке полумрак,
разъезд с работы, мартовская муть,
присутствие реки за два квартала,
и я уже хочу, чтоб что-нибудь
нас от беседы нашей оторвало,
но продолжаю говорить про долг,
про крест, но он уже далече.

It all was neither fish nor fowl, but verbiage
let down with limpness so it turned to mush;
but all the same, from time to time I managed
to print this nonsense. God will be my judge.

Frost. In the Tauride Garden, sunset stripe
showed yellow, and the snow beneath was rosy.
And people's idle chatter as they stride
was monitored by vigilant Morózov –
Pavlik, the one who did that evil deed.
The chipboard portrait of this Pioneer
has chipped off from the cold, but still, indeed
they have it cosy.
                Time went on ahead.
The first day of another month approached, and
the secretary counts out our paltry screw.
And time went on, begging nobody's pardon,
and landed everyone in a different do.
Now, some get stoned on strong tea in the GULag,
some in the Bronx make war upon the roach;
in mental homes yet others cluck and cuckoo,
brushing the baby devils from their coats.

VI

My best friend was a semi-foe as well,
a man who would not make his bed, not ever.
You won't believe this, but we'd talked together
the whole day through. Now, semi-darkness fell;
end of the working day, the murk of March,
two blocks away the ever-present river,
me wishing now that something would deliver
us from the non-stop natter, but I marched
ahead, saying my piece on ethics, ought-tos,
bearing one's cross – but he had gone adrift.

Он, руки накрест, взял себя за плечи
и съежился, как будто он продрог.
И этим совершенно женским жестом
он отвергает мой простой резон.
Как проницательно заметил Гершензон:
«Ущербное одноприродно с совершенством».

VII

Покуда Мельпомена и Евтерпа
настраивали дудочки свои,
и дирижер выныривал, как нерпа,
из светлой оркестровой полыньи,
и дрейфовал на сцене, как на льдине,
пингвином принаряженный солист,
и бегала старушка-капельдинер
с листовками, как старый нигилист,
улавливая ухом труляля,
я в то же время погружался взглядом
в мерцающую груду хрусталя,
нависшую застывшим водопадом:
там умирал последний огонек,
и я его спасти уже не мог.

На сцене барин корчил мужика,
тряслась кулиса, лампочка мигала,
и музыка, как будто мы — зека,
командовала нами, помыкала,
на сцене дама руки изломала,
она в ушах производила звон,
она производила в душах шмон
и острые предметы изымала.

Послы, министры, генералитет
застыли в ложах. Смолкли разговоры.

With arms across and hands gripping his shoulders,
he sat there hunched, like someone frozen stiff.
This purely female gesture quite undid
the straight line of my argument's direction.
I thought of what wise Gershenzon once said:
'Deficiency is cognate with perfection'.

VII

Euterpe and Melpomene would meanwhile
be tuning up their tooting instruments,
then up would bob the maestro like a sealion
out of the icehole that the spotlight melts,
a soloist all spiffed up like a penguin
slides to position on the stage's floe,
while busily the old crone kappeldiener
hands broadsheets out, like nihilist of yore;
I register this tra-la-la, but meantime
a different object holds my eyes in thrall:
that twinkling crystalline inverted mountain,
that cascade frozen high above the stalls,
whose final spark of light was soon to die,
and nothing I can do will make it stay.

On stage a squire pretends to be a peasant,
the backdrop twitches, light follows the dark,
the music marches us away to prison,
deprives us of our rights, puts us to work;
the heroine wrings her hands (right to the shoulders),
puts bells into our ears and makes them ring,
performs a strip-search of our hearts and souls, and
confiscates each and every sharp-edged thing.

The generals and the ministers and the statesmen
stiff in their boxes. Conversation dies.

Буфетчица читала «Алитет
уходит в горы». Снег. Уходит в горы.
Салфетка. Глетчер. Мраморный буфет.
Хрусталь – фужеры. Снежные заторы.
И льдинками украшенных конфет
с медведями пред ней лежали горы.
Как я любил холодные просторы
пустых фойе в начале января,
когда ревет сопрано: «Я твоя!»,
и солнце гладит бархатные шторы.

Там, за окном, в Михайловском саду
лишь снегири в суворовских мундирах,
два льва при них гуляют в командирах
с нашлепкой снега – здесь и на заду.
А дальше – заторошена Нева,
Карелия и Баренцева лужа,
откуда к нам приходит эта стужа,
что нашего основа естества.
Все, как задумал медный наш творец, –
у нас чем холоднее, тем интимней,
когда растаял Ледяной дворец,
мы навсегда другой воздвигли – Зимний.

И все же, откровенно говоря,
от оперного мерного прибоя
мне кажется порою с перепоя –
нужны России теплые моря!

НЕЛЕТНАЯ ПОГОДА

Где некий храм струился в небеса,
теперь там головешки, кучки кала
и узкая канала полоса,

The bargirl reads her agitprop-escapist
novel. But no escape from snow and ice.
Napkin. Ice bucket. Buffet iced with marble.
Frosty tall glasses. Snowy pinafores.
A rounded heap of glacier mints, their wrappers
with polar bear on iceberg, lies before.
Oh, how I used to love the chill wide spaces
of foyers bare in January's first days,
and the soprano screech: 'My dearest, take me',
while sunshine strokes the plush of window drapes.

Outside, sole guardians of the Michael Garden –
bullfinches, in Suvórov uniform;
two lions, paw-up, strut like their commanders,
with pats of snow up here and on the rump.
Behind, Neva clapped up in chains for winter,
Karelia, Barents puddle not that far,
the source that sends us down this freezing weather –
the basic fact that makes us what we are.
Things stay the way our bronze creator made them;
the colder we, the closer our embrace;
an Ice Palace was built, and when it melted,
we raised the Winter one to take its place.

But all the same, and now I really mean it,
the measured ebb and flow of opera leads
to thinking – if I've had a drop too many –
that warm seas are what Russia really needs!

GROUNDED

Where once a church streamed upwards to the skies,
now lie charred embers, piles of excrement;
where once upon a time the Výtegra

где Вытегра когда-то вытекала
из озера. Тихонечко бася,
ползет буксир. Накрапывает дрема.
Последняя на область колбаса
повисла на шесте аэродрома.
Пилот уже с утра залил глаза
и дрыхнет, завернувшись в плащ-палатку.
Сегодня нам не улететь. Коза
общипывает взлетную площадку.
Спроси пилота, ну зачем он пьет,
он ничего ответить не сумеет.
Ну, дождик. Отменяется полет.
Ну, дождик сеет. Ну, коза не блеет.

Коза молчит и думает свое,
и взглядом пожелтелым от люцерны
она низводит наземь воронье,
освобождая небеса от скверны,
и тут же превращает птичью рать
в немытых пэтэушников команду.
Их тянет на пожарище пожрать,
пожарить девок, потравить баланду.
Как много их шагает сквозь туман,
бутылки под шинелками припрятав,
как много среди юных россиян
страдающих поносом геростратов.

Кто в этом нас посмеет укорить —
что погорели, не дойдя до цели.

Пилот проснулся. Хочется курить.
Есть беломор. Но спички отсырели.

flowed from the lake, there's nothing but a thin
strip of canal. With sotto voce bass
a tugboat crawls. Drowsiness patters down.
The very last piece of sausage in the region
is hanging from the pole out on the airfield.
The pilot got blind pissed first thing this morning
and snores away wrapped in his army cape.
We won't be getting off today. A goat
stands there and nibbles at the landing strip.
You ask the pilot why he needs to drink,
and not a single reason can he give.
The bloody rain. The bloody flight delays.
Down the rain beats. The bloody goat can't bleat.

The goat is silent, thinking its own thoughts;
with eyes turned yellow by the lucerne grass
it calls a flock of crows down to the earth,
thus liberating heaven from this blight,
and metamorphosing that wingèd host
into a gang of unwashed tech-school kids.
To this burned-out place they come to stuff themselves,
then stuff some local girls, then pull some stunts.
So many of them, striding through the mist,
their bottles stashed away beneath their coats.
So many of these young Russians hereabouts:
Herostrates with diarrhoea, they are.

But who would dare admonish us for this –
for burning out before we reached our goal?

The pilot's woken up. He wants a smoke.
Damp matches will not light his Belomór.

ПОСЛЕДНИЙ РОМАНС
Юзу Алешковскому

> Не слышно шуму городского,
> В заневских башнях тишина!
>   Ф. Глинка

Над невской башней тишина.
Она опять позолотела.
Вот едет женщина одна.
Она опять подзалетела.

Все отражает лунный лик,
воспетый сонмищем поэтов, —
не только часового штык,
но много колющих предметов.

Блеснет Адмиралтейства шприц,
и местная анестезия
вмиг проморозит до границ
то место, где была Россия.

Окоченение к лицу
не только в чреве недоноску,
но и его недоотцу,
с утра упившемуся в доску.

Подходит недорождество,
мертво от недостатка елок.
В стране пустых небес и полок
уж не родится ничего.

Мелькает мертвый Летний сад.
Вот едет женщина назад.
Ее искусаны уста.
И башня невская пуста.

THE LAST ROMANCE
for Yuz Aleshkovsky

> The city noise can not be heard,
> In Neva tower silence reigns!
> FËDOR GLINKA

Silence hangs o'er Neva's grim tower.
And yet again, its gilding's slick.
Here comes a woman all alone.
And yet again, she's up the stick.

The moon's round face reflects all that,
as sung by endless hosts of poets:
not just the sentry's bayonet
but many other things with points.

The Admiralty needle glints,
and local anaesthetic seeps,
instantly freezing all it hits –
the place where Russia used to be.

This state of numbness suits them fine:
the aborted foetus on its way,
the aborted father full of wine
who's been blind drunk since break of day.

Miscarried Christmas soon arrives;
shortage of firs for party mirth.
This land of empty skies and shelves
will not bring anything to birth.

The Summer Garden's died the death.
Back goes that woman, feeling ill,
with bloodied lips, and out of breath.
The Neva tower is empty still.

ОН ГОВОРИЛ: «А ЭТО БАЗИЛИК»

Он говорил: «А это базилик».
И с грядки на английскую тарелку –
румяную редиску, лука стрелку,
и пес вихлялся, вывалив язык.
Он по-простому звал меня – Алеха.
«Давай еще, по-русски, под пейзаж».
Нам стало хорошо. Нам стало плохо.
Залив был Финский. Это значит наш.

О, родина с великой буквы Р,
вернее, С, вернее *Еръ* несносный,
бессменный воздух наш орденоносный
и почва – инвалид и кавалер.
Простые имена – Упырь, Редедя,
союз ц/ч/з/ека, быка и мужика,
лес имени товарища Медведя,
луг имени товарища Жука.

В Сибири ястреб уронил слезу.
В Москве взошел на кафедру былинка.
Ругнулись сверху. Пукнули внизу.
Задребезжал фарфор, и вышел Глинка.
Конь-Пушкин, закусивший удила,
сей китоврас, восславивший свободу.
Давали воблу – тысяча народу.
Давали «Сильву». Дуська не дала.

И родина пошла в тартарары.
Теперь там холод, грязь и комары.
Пес умер, да и друг уже не тот.
В дом кто-то новый въехал торопливо.
И ничего, конечно, не растет
на грядке возле бывшего залива.

'AND THIS ONE HERE IS BASIL', HE DECLARED

'And this one here is basil', he declared.
Onto an English china plate he lowered
some reddish radish and a spear of scallion.
His pooch loped round about, lolling tongue bared.
He called me, like a peasant would, 'Alyokha'.
'Let's have another, Russian style, out here'.
We felt just fine at first. Then we felt awful.
The Gulf of Finland (i.e. ours) curved near.

O native realm with great big capital R,
or rather S – or rather, loathsome 'are';
the stagnant air bedecked with medal bars,
the soil serving as warrior and squire.
Those simple names such as Upýr, Redédya,
Union of co(m/n/p)s, cattle, and country folk,
forest in memory of Comrade Bruin,
and meadow in memory of Comrade Bug.

A hawk east of the Urals shed a tear.
A frail stem rose to give a talk in Moscow.
An oath rang out above. A fart beneath.
The china rattled and rang out as Glinka.
Pushkin the frisky stallion felt his oats,
a fishnorfowl who sang in praise of freedom.
Smoked fish they rationed out to feed the people.
They put out 'Silva'. Duska didn't put out.

That motherland is stuck far up shit creek.
These days it's naught but frost and filth and skeets.
The pooch is dead, my friend's beyond recall.
A stranger lost no time taking his kingdom.
And growing now – you guessed – is bugger all
in garden plot by the ex-Gulf of Finland.

NOTES TO THE ENGLISH TEXTS

[pp. 24-5 'At the Clinic': This poem was published in Russian and translated after the poet's death; it was evidently written too late for inclusion in his last collection.]

pp. 26-7 'An Excursion': On the Boundary Canal in Leningrad / St. Petersburg – see 'The Tram' (in section VII).

pp. 30-1 'School No. 1': The poem refers to the atrocity at the school in Beslan (Chechnya) in September 2004.

pp. 32-3 'Joseph in 1965': 'and mended those tatty roofs' is a reference to one of the poems Joseph Brodsky wrote about carrying out physical labour during his administrative exile in Arkhangelsk province in 1964-5.

pp. 42-3 'Grounded Again': The poem refers to the author's earlier poem 'Grounded' (see pp. 138-9).

pp. 44-5 'The Funeral Parlour's Abuzz...': The poem refers to the funeral of Joseph Brodsky in Greenwich Village in January, 1996.

pp. 46-7 S. D.: The initials are those of the writer Sergei Dovlatov (1941-90), who grew up in Leningrad and emigrated to the USA in 1978. Aleksei Stakhanov was a coal miner who in 1935 exceeded his daily output quota fourteen-fold (102 tons of coal instead of 7). He, or rather his Party handlers, started the 'Stakhanovite' movement in the USSR. Stakhanov was celebrated as a Hero of Socialist Labour. It was rumoured that he took to drinking heavily, and died from alcohol-related illness.

pp. 48-9 'Out of Bunin': This poem was inspired by Ivan Bunin's novella *Light Breathing* (Legkoe dykhanie, 1916).

pp. 58-9 'June 1972': The month of June 1972 was exceptionally hot in Russia, with continuous forest and peat-bog fires. On 2 June 1972 Joseph Brodsky left the country, never to return. The phrase 'Period of Stagnation' is commonly used in Russian to refer to the Brezhnev years, between Khrushchev and Gorbachev.

pp. 60-1 'Dostoevsky's Handwriting': 'No way to confine it' alludes to the words of Dmitrii Karamazov, 'No, man is broad, even too broad – I would narrow him down' (*The Brothers Karamazov,* Book 3, Chapter 3).

pp. 66-7 'Afterword' – Author's Note: "In the preface to my first book, *The Miraculous Raid* (1985), I said that the stimulus for my creative writing was Joseph Brodsky's departure from Russia in 1972. It was as if some compensatory mechanisms had kicked in: no longer the direct witness of Joseph's creative activity, without noticing anything I started writing my own poetry. I wrote as the Lord commanded, with no thought not only of publishing the results, but even of showing anything to the people closest to me. At an almost unconscious level there was from the very beginning, though, one limitation, which was that if anything in a poem in progress smacked of Brodsky – his tone of voice, vocabulary, wit – it was thrown out. It wasn't a matter of that notorious 'anxiety of influence', but of the obvious indelicacy, even comic absurdity, that would have resulted from combining elements of Brodsky's refined and tragic manner with what I was writing.

A few weeks after Joseph's death on 28 January 1996 a cycle of poems started coming to me that were directly or indirectly connected with his memory (what he called 'poetry's memorial fragments' [used in a famous elegy by Vladimir Mayakovsky]), and in this cycle, contrary to my rule, there was a lot that was his – words, tones of voice, sometimes direct quotations. This now seemed somehow appropriate, perhaps because at the same time I often dreamed about him, and between dream and poem there is a stronger connection than people think. The poems of this period make up the first section of 'Afterword'.

Later, the tide of borrowings started to ebb, at the same time as the grief of loss started to ebb, and emptiness has gone on growing in the place where Brodsky ought to have been.

18 November 1997, Hanover, New Hampshire"

pp. 68-9 'Cold (1921-1996)': Vladimir Veidle was a highly regarded émigré critic and literary scholar. He wrote a long essay on what he called 'Petersburg poetics', discussing what there was in common between the younger generation of Russian Symbolists, whose undisputed leader was Aleksandr Blok (1880-1921), and their successors, who called themselves Acmeists. The poetry of the former in many ways may be compared to that of Yeats, while the latter, in whose ranks were such poets as Anna Akhmatova and Osip Mandelshtam and whose main spokesman was Nikolai Gumilev, professed ideas very similar to those of the Anglo-American Imagists. Forty-year-old Blok and Gumilev, who was thirty-five, died almost simultaneously: one from illness exacerbated by the privations of the Civil War period, the other executed by the Bolsheviks for alleged conspiracy against their regime. From Veidle's point of view the normal development of Russian poetry was interrupted for the next four decades until the young Brodsky in the early 1960s began writing in the same vein as the poets of Blok and Gumilev's epoch. 'Lorry engines': During executions in the courtyard of the Cheka building or in the killing fields outside the city, the operatives would gun the engines of their lorries to muffle the shots and the cries of the victims.

pp. 70-1 "The chevelure of Petersburg columns...": Kamaz is an acronym of Kamskii avtomobil´nyi zavod (Kama Automobile Factory), where big trucks were produced. 'Smerdyakóv': Smerdyakóv, the name of the character from *The Brothers Karamazov,* is evocative of the verb *smerdet´,* "to stink".

pp. 74-5 "Where the air itself is 'pink-tinged from the pantiles'...": The last two lines of the original contain a play on words: the Russian for Sunday, *voskresen´e,* is homonymous with the word for 'Resurrection'.

pp. 80-1 'In Memory of Mikhail Krasilnikov': Krasilnikov (1933-98) was a 'neo-Futurist' poet, and the charismatic leader of a group of young poets in Leningrad in the 1950s. From 1956-60 he was in prison for 'anti-Soviet activity'. He lived the remainder of his life in Riga, Latvia. [Loseff has also published 'Mikhail Krasilnikov: A Memoir', *Ulbandus Review,* 9 (2005-6), 69-86.]

pp. 80-1 'Me and the Old Lady': the poem is set at Norwich University in Northfield, Vermont, where for many years a Russian summer school was held.

pp. 88-9 'For O's Scrapbook': 'One star conversing with another' is a paraphrase of a line from Mikhail Lermontov's famous lyric 'Alone I walked out on the road'; this is not the only allusion to this poem here. Bulat Okudzhava (1924-97) was a poet and balladeer; this poem was written in response to a request by his wife Olga to write something in her scrapbook, when the Okudzhavas and the author were spending the summer in Northfield, Vermont.

pp. 94-5 'The Parisian Note': A motley group of young Russian émigré poets who lived in Paris between the two world wars was known by this term; they followed the precepts of the critic Georgii Adamovich, who called for the renunciation of grand themes. Many of them perished during World War II; some committed suicide. The phrase '...vraiment ça finit mal' paraphrases a line by Paul Verlaine.

pp. 96-7 'There but for...' (15 June 1925): The author was born on 15 June, but in 1937.

pp. 102-3 'Toilette': The poem is an accurate description of my mother's mahogany Empire dressing-table as I remember it in 1944-5. It looked very out of place in our small crowded room in a communal apartment. There was, incongruously, a cheap Soviet radio (the 'black platter made of paper') on the wall above it that played 'The International' at midnight and 6 a.m., until 1944 when the new anthem was introduced. The two lines of dots in the poem separate the topsy-turvy world beyond the looking glass from real life back in the room.

pp. 104-5 'Ledger Entry': The inmates of Soviet prisons and prison camps were not allowed to use the normal mode of address, 'Comrade', when speaking to their guards, but had to say 'Citizen' instead, e.g. 'Citizen Commander! Permission to go to the toilet?' For situations when by a slip of the tongue a prisoner would address them as 'Comrade', court officials and prison guards had a set reply: 'I am no comrade to you. Your comrade is the Tambov wolf!'

pp. 106-7 'December Dreams Come in a Crazy Rush': 'Piter' is a colloquial nickname for the city of St Petersburg. At the time this poem was written, M. M. Meilakh, a Russian literary scholar, was serving a 5-year sentence for anti-Soviet activity in the Perm prison camp, known for the especially harsh treatment of political prisoners.

pp. 112-3 'The Tram': From 1947-63 I lived with my parents on Mozháiskaia St in Leningrad, one block from the Bypass (*Obvódnyi*) Canal, a stinking industrially-polluted waterway. One could see lots of used condoms and the occasional dead animal floating in it. Tram tickets had six-digit numbers on them. If the sum of the first three numbers equalled the sum of the last three, it was thought to be lucky.

pp. 114-5 'I'm Living in the States From Boredom': Nikolai Glazkov was a poet, and my drinking buddy in the summer of 1958. Oleg Tselkov, an artist and old friend, has lived in France since 1975. In *Evgenii Onegin,* Chapter 8, stanza LI, Pushkin quotes from the thirteenth-century Persian poet Sa'adi: 'Some are far distant, some are dead' (tr. Charles Johnston).

pp. 120-1 'Sonnet': The 'monument built of brick' is 9 Griboedov Canal, a building in Leningrad where the author once lived. Numerous writers and scholars have lived in apartments there, including Zoshchenko, Eikhenbaum, and Tomashevsky. The diabetic writer sitting in the square is the author's father. Just across the canal from the building is a park with a monument to Pushkin, in front of the Russian Museum. The statue of Lenin atop an armoured car stands in front of the Finland Station. [It was damaged by a bomb on 1 April 2009.]

pp. 124-5 'The Extended Day': 'The Extended Day' was the programme for schoolchildren whose parents wanted them to remain in school after classes. [pp. 126-7]'... allied with Nelson, instead of face a hole...': Street photographers used to have life-sized pictures of dashing horsemen painted on plywood with a hole cut out in place of the face. One could stand behind, stick one's face into the hole, and be photographed as the brave warrior on horseback with sabre in hand. Here, a young boy's dream of becoming a great admiral is compared to sticking his chubby bespectacled face in similar holes but in the portraits of famous sea captains. [pp. 127-8] 'A play by Shvarts': In fantasy plays such as *The Dragon* by Evgenii Shvarts (1896-1958) there were many *double-entendre* jokes in which the sophisticated audience could recognize jabs at the Soviet regime. [pp. 128-9] '...to catch a troika...', i.e. a No. 3 tram, by St Michael's Castle. [pp. 128-9] The author lived on Prospekt Gaza as a nine-year-old, in 1946-7; its old name, Staropetergofskii Prospekt, has now been restored. In Soviet times the street was named after Ivan Gaza, an Estonian Bolshevik and revolutionary hero. [pp. 130-1] '...as taught by Lotman...': Yurii Mikhailovich Lotman (1922-93), the most important figure in the history of Russian structuralism and semiotics. His most widely read book was *The Structure of the Artistic Text* (1970). Lotman was genuinely amused by this poem, and communicated his impression to the author in 1990 at the International Conference of Slavists, in Harrogate, Yorkshire. [pp. 132-3] Pavel (Pavlik) Morózov was a Soviet propaganda icon: a young Pioneer, he informed on his own father, and was martyred by "the reactionary peasants". [pp. 134-5] '... wise Gershenzón...': M.O. Gershenzon (1869-1925), a Russian philosopher and cultural historian.

pp. 138-9 'Grounded': Výtegra is a small provincial river and town. Belomór (from 'Belomorkanal', 'The White Sea Canal'), the brand of Soviet *papirosa* introduced to commemorate Stalin's monstrous engineering project of 1934, and retaining their trademark blue packet to the present day.

pp. 142-3 '"And this one here is basil", he declared': 'The china rattled...': a hidden quotation from a collective poem written by Pushkin and others on the occasion of the première of Mikhail Glinka's opera *A Life for the Tsar* (*Ivan Susanin*, 1836). A line in the poem puns on Glinka's name, which means 'clay': 'He isn't *glinka* anymore, but porcelain!'. 'A fishnorfowl': the original has *kitovras,* the Old Russian word for 'centaur'; Pushkin is compared to a sacred monster, wise and powerful. *Silva (Die Csardasfürstin)* is an operetta by Imre Kalman. It was very popular in the USSR during the Second World War and the lean post-war years. Starving and shabbily dressed audiences went to theatres to indulge in reveries about champagne-drinking men clad in tails and women glittering with diamonds.

BIOGRAPHICAL NOTES

LEV LOSEFF writes:
"I was born (in 1937) and grew up in Leningrad, and graduated from the Department of Journalism in the Faculty of Philology at Leningrad State University. For a short time I worked on a newspaper in northern Sakhalin, and then, from 1962 to 1975, I was an editor on *The Campfire*, a magazine for children. I wrote plays for the puppet theatre, poetry for children, and things like that. To avoid confusion, my father, the well-known children's writer and poet Vladimir Lifshits, invented the pseudonym 'Losev' for me. After I moved to America in 1976 I made this former pseudonym my legal name (Lev Lifschutz Loseff).

In America I worked as a compositor and proofreader for the Ardis publishing house, took my Ph.D. at the University of Michigan, and since 1979 I have been teaching Russian literature at Dartmouth College in northern New England. I have published a book about Aesopian language in Soviet literature and a large number of articles, mainly about Russian poetry.

I wrote some lyric poetry when I was a student, but I had doubts about its originality and abandoned it. I began writing this poetry again, to my own surprise, in 1974, and have been publishing it since 1979, at first in émigré journals, and then from 1988 in Russia."

From *Collected. Poems, Prose* (Ekaterinburg, 2000)

Lev Loseff died in Hanover, New Hampshire, USA, on 6 May 2009. In 2011, his copiously annotated two-volume edition of the poetry of Joseph Brodsky was published in the prestigious 'New Poet's Library' series in St. Petersburg. His uniquely authoritative biography of Brodsky, published in Russia in 2006, came out in Jane Ann Miller's translation as *Joseph Brodsky: A Literary Life* in 2011 from Yale University Press.

GERALD STANTON SMITH is Professor Emeritus of Russian in the University of Oxford and Emeritus Fellow of New College. His book-length translations from Russian include the poetry of Alexander Galich (Ardis, 1983) and Boris Slutsky (glas, 1996), and *Contemporary Russian Poetry: A Bilingual Anthology* (Indiana University Press, 1993). With Marina Tarlinskaja he translated M. L. Gasparov, *A History of European Versification* (Clarendon Press, 1996). His award-winning biography of D. S. Mirsky was published by Oxford University Press in 2000, and a translated selection of his articles on Russian poetry, *Vzgliad izvne*, by Yazyki slavianskoi kul'tury (Moscow) in 2002.

BARRY P SCHERR, Professor of Russian at Dartmouth College in Hanover, New Hampshire, has written widely on twentieth-century Russian literature and on Russian verse theory. His books include *Russian Poetry: Meter, Rhythm, and Rhyme*; *A Sense of Place: Tsarskoe Selo and Its Poets* (co-edited with Lev Loseff); *Maksim Gorky: Selected Letters* (co-edited and co-translated with Andrew Barratt); and, with Nicholas Luker, *The Shining World: Exploring Aleksandr Grin's Grinlandia*.

Also available in the Arc Publications
'VISIBLE POETS' SERIES (Series Editor: Jean Boase-Beier)

No. 1 – MIKLÓS RADNÓTI (Hungary)
Camp Notebook
Translated by Francis Jones, introduced by George Szirtes

No. 2 – BARTOLO CATTAFI (Italy)
Anthracite
Translated by Brian Cole, introduced by Peter Dale
(Poetry Book Society Recommended Translation)

No. 3 – MICHAEL STRUNGE (Denmark)
A Virgin from a Chilly Decade
Translated by Bente Elsworth, introduced by John Fletcher

No. 4 – TADEUSZ RÓZEWICZ (Poland)
recycling
Translated by Barbara Bogoczek (Plebanek) & Tony Howard,
introduced by Adam Czerniawski

No. 5 – CLAUDE DE BURINE (France)
Words Have Frozen Over
Translated by Martin Sorrell, introduced by Susan Wicks

No. 6 – CEVAT ÇAPAN (Turkey)
Where Are You, Susie Petschek?
Translated by Cevat Çapan & Michael Hulse,
introduced by A. S. Byatt

No. 7 – JEAN CASSOU (France)
33 Sonnets of the Resistance
With an original introduction by Louis Aragon
Translated by Timothy Adès, introduced by Alistair Elliot

No. 8 – ARJEN DUINKER (Holland)
The Sublime Song of a Maybe
Translated by Willem Groenewegen, introduced by Jeffrey Wainwright

No. 9 – MILA HAUGOVÁ (Slovakia)
Scent of the Unseen
Translated by James & Viera Sutherland-Smith,
introduced by Fiona Sampson

No. 10 – ERNST MEISTER (Germany)
Between Nothing and Nothing
Translated by Jean Boase-Beier, introduced by John Hartley Williams

No. 11 – YANNIS KONDOS (Greece)
Absurd Athlete
Translated by David Connolly, introduced by David Constantine

No. 12 – BEJAN MATUR (Turkey)
In the Temple of a Patient God
Translated by Ruth Christie, introduced by Maureen Freely

No. 13 – GABRIEL FERRATER (Catalonia / Spain)
Women and Days
Translated by Arthur Terry, introduced by Seamus Heaney

No. 14 – INNA LISNIANSKAYA (Russia)
Far from Sodom
Translated by Daniel Weissbort, introduced by Elaine Feinstein
(Poetry Book Society Recommended Translation)

No. 15 – SABINE LANGE (Germany)
The Fishermen Sleep
Translated by Jenny Williams, introduced by Mary O'Donnell

No. 16 – TAKAHASHI MUTSUO (Japan)
We of Zipangu
Translated by James Kirkup & Tamaki Makoto, introduced by Glyn Pursglove

No. 17 – JURIS KRONBERGS (Latvia)
Wolf One-Eye
Translated by Mara Rozitis, introduced by Jaan Kaplinski

No. 18 – REMCO CAMPERT (Holland)
I Dreamed in the Cities at Night
Translated by Donald Gardner, introduced by Paul Vincent

No. 19 – DOROTHEA ROSA HERLIANY (Indonesia)
Kill the Radio
Translated by Harry Aveling, introduced by Linda France

No. 20 – SOLEÏMAN ADEL GUÉMAR (Algeria)
State of Emergency
Translated by Tom Cheesman & John Goodby, introduced by Lisa Appignanesi
(PEN Translation Award)

No. 21 – ELI TOLARETXIPI (Spain / Basque)
Still Life with Loops
Translated by Philip Jenkins, introduced by Robert Crawford

No. 22 – FERNANDO KOFMAN (Argentina)
The Flights of Zarza
Translated by Ian Taylor, introduced by Andrew Graham Yooll

No. 23 – LARISSA MILLER (Russia)
Guests of Eternity
Translated by Richard McKane, introduced by Sasha Dugdale
(Poetry Book Society Recommended Translation)

No. 24 – ANISE KOLTZ (Luxembourg)
At the Edge of Night
Translated by Anne-Marie Glasheen, introduced by Caroline Price

No. 25 – MAURICE CARÊME (Belgium)
Defying Fate
Translated by Christopher Pilling, introduced by Martin Sorrell

No. 26 – VALÉRIE ROUZEAU (France)
Cold Spring in Winter
Translated by Susan Wicks, introduced by Stephen Romer
(Short-listed, Griffin Poetry Prize, 2010 &
Oxford-Weidenfeld Translation Prize, 2010)

No. 27 – RAZMIK DAVOYAN (France)
Whispers and Breath of the Meadows
Translated by Arminé Tamrazian, introduced by W. N. Herbert

No. 28 – FRANÇOIS JACQMIN (Belgium)
The Book of the Snow
Translated by Philip Mosley, introduced by Clive Scott

No. 29 – KRISTIINA EHIN (Estonia)
The Scent of Your Shadow
Translated by Ilmar Lehtpere, introduced by Sujata Bhatt
(Poetry Book Society Recommended Translation)

No. 30 – META KUŠAR (Slovenia)
Ljubljana
Translated by Ana Jelnikar & Stephen Watts, introduced by Francis R. Jones

No. 31 – LUDWIG STEINHERR (Germany)
Before the Invention of Paradise
Translated by Richard Dove, introduced by Jean Boase-Beier

No. 32 – FABIO PUSTERLA (Switzerland)
Days Full of Caves and Tigers
Translated by Simon Knight, introduced by Alan Brownjohn